STOC HOLM

⊙ Walking Eye App

Your guide now includes a free eBook to your chosen destination, for the same great price as before. Simply download the Walking Eye App from the App Store or Google Play to access your free eBook.

HOW THE WALKING EYE APP WORKS

Through the Walking Eye App, you can purchase a range of eBooks and destination content. However, when you buy this book, you can download the corresponding eBook for free. Just see below in the grey panel where to find your free content and then scan the QR code at the bottom of this page.

Destinations: Download essential destination content featuring recommended sights and attractions, restaurants, hotels and an A–Z of practical information, all available for purchase.

Ships: Interested in ship reviews? Find independent reviews of river and ocean ships in this section, all available for purchase.

eBooks: You can download your free accompanying digital version of this guide here. You will also find a whole range of other eBooks, all available for purchase.

Free access to travel-related blog articles about different destinations, updated on a daily basis.

HOW THE EBOOKS WORK

The eBooks are provided in EPUB file format. Please note that you will need an eBook reader installed on your device to open the file. Many devices come with this as standard, but you may still need to install one manually from Google Play.

The eBook content is identical to the content in the printed guide.

HOW TO DOWNLOAD THE WALKING EYE APP

1. Download the Walking Eye App from the App Store or Google Play.
2. Open the app and select the scanning function from the main menu.
3. Scan the QR code on this page – you will then be asked a security question to verify ownership of the book.
4. Once this has been verified, you will see your eBook in the purchased ebook section, where you will be able to download it.

Other destination apps and eBooks are available for purchase separately or are free with the purchase of the Insight Guide book.

CONTENTS

CITY VIEWS

Climb the stairs up the Stadshuset tower (route 1), walk along Fjällgatan with views of Saltsjön (route 7) or take the lift to rooftop restaurant Gondolen, one of the best in the city (route 7).

RECOMMENDED ROUTES FOR...

CHILDREN

Kids will love the fun amusement park Gröna Lund Tivoli (route 4), Astrid Lindgren's glorious fairy-tale world at Junibacken (route 4), and making their own inventions at Tekniskamuseet (route 6).

ESCAPING THE CROWDS

For a more subdued day, venture out to the islands. Vaxholm (route 12), Utö (route 16) and Fjäderholmarna (route 11) all offer lots of things to do away from the city crowds.

MUSEUM BUFFS

The museum islands of Djurgården (route 4) and Blasieholmen–Skeppsholmen (route 3) feature an incredible variety of museums. Also find dazzling artefacts at the Hallwylska Museet and the Historiska Museet (route 6).

MUSIC LOVERS

Enjoy classical music or opera at Konserthuset (route 2) or Kungliga Operan (route 3). If pop is more your scene, visit ABBA: the Museum (route 4).

PARKS AND GARDENS

For a spot of greenery, visit the stunning terraces of Millesgården (route 10), the vast city park of Hagaparken (route 9) or the eastern end of Djurgården (route 5) with wide open spaces to explore.

ROYAL STOCKHOLM

Have a right royal time at the Kungliga Slottet (route 1). Or get out into the country at Rosendals Slott (route 5), Drottningholms Slott (route 8) and Ulriksdals Slott (route 9).

WORLD HERITAGE SITES

Stockholm's Unesco World Heritage Sites include Drottningholm (route 8), a smaller Nordic version of Versailles, and Birka (route 13), which travels back in time to the Viking Age with extensive 8th-century excavations.

INTRODUCTION

An introduction to Stockholm's geography, customs and culture, plus illuminating background information on cuisine, history and what to do when you're there.

Cobbled street in Gamla Stan

EXPLORE STOCKHOLM

Sweden's capital is a city of islands, where palaces and peaceful hideaways line the shores, green spaces punctuate the cityscape and cobbled streets lead to traditional cafés, sleek modern restaurants, and lively cultural attractions.

At Stockholm's heart is the water, from its earliest times as a trading port, its naval importance and through to the present day as a magnet for tourism. Boats and bridges link island to island, allowing visitors to wander at will from the cobbled streets of Gamla Stan (Old Town) to the buzzing cafés and clubs of Södermalm. All this water adds to the charm of Stockholm, whether you sail to enchanting Drottningholms Slott, slip back in time at the Viking-era settlement Birka, or visit the Vasa Museum to marvel at its glittering golden warship.

GEOGRAPHY AND LAYOUT

Dramatically situated at a point where the Baltic and the waters of Lake Mälaren collide, the city has been splendidly endowed by nature. Described by Swedish novelist Selma Lagerlöf as 'the city that floats on water', only the city centre to the north is situated on the mainland, with the rest of it spread gracefully, if unevenly, over 14 islands that are connected by no fewer than 40 bridges.

Fresh and salt water are separated by the island of Gamla Stan and the great lock gates of Slussen at the southern end. This island barrier is where Stockholm emerged some time before the 13th century. To the east are the thousands of islands of the archipelago, numbering nearly 30,000. Hundreds of small boats bobbing along the edge of the inlets and islands are testament to the passion of every Stockholm family to own and sail a boat.

Getting around
Stockholm is fairly compact and the main attractions easy to cover by foot. The public transport system is excellent and the city is served by an efficient metro, bus and tram service. Many attractions and the outlying islands are accessible by ferry or by organised boat trips, most of which are summer only. Unusually for a capital city traffic flows relatively freely, even during rush hour, and many locals use bicycles to get around.

ARCHITECTURE

The oldest buildings in the city are located at Gamla Stan. It was on this island of antiquity at the heart of the city, around 1252, that Stockholm was born. Here you will find perfectly preserved 15th- and

Summer at Skansen   *Waterside view of Kungliga Palace*

16th-century houses and the Kungliga Slott (Royal Palace), the oldest parts dating from the 1660s. Here, too, is the awesome Gothic cathedral, Storkyrkan, dating back to the 13th century, the oldest church in Gamla Stan, and the scene of many royal occasions and coronations. In stark contrast is the modern city centre, the northern sector of town and location of Sergels Torg with its glass and steel skyscrapers, malls, underpasses and roundabouts, which has both feet planted firmly in the late 20th century.

Developments for the 21st century

Stockholm is seeing a boom in building and has more than 100 active and planned projects for new structures and renovations of existing neighbourhoods. The massive junction at Sluseen is undergoing major development to transform it into a safe and efficient junction for pedestrians, cyclists and public transport. New public open spaces, walkways and restaurants will transform an ugly traffic hub into a cool new urban environment. Always at the heart of these projects are the environmental impact on the city and Stockholm was the first recipient of the EU's European Green Capital award in 2010. Green space and fresh air is paramount to Stockholmers and a trip to the city's Ekoparken (see box) is high on the agenda at the weekend.

CLIMATE

Summer is the prime season to visit Stockholm, with temperatures rising above 20°C (70°F) and lots of sunshine and daylight lasting up to 19 hours, but it does mean there are lots of tourists too. In dazzling spring and autumn with its bright colours and clear nights, you'll find far less visitors. Winter is tempting for sports enthusiasts and Christmas

Royal National Park

Ekoparken (www.nationalstadsparken. se) is the world's first national park, a mighty set of green lungs stretching out in a 12km (7-mile) long arch, from Ulriksdals Slott (Ulriksdal Palace) in the north to the archipelago islands of Fjäderholmarna in the south, encompassing three royal parks: Djurgården, Haga and Uriksdal.

The feature that distinguishes Ekoparken from other European city parks is its wildness – large tracts of historical parklands and untamed wilderness intersect throughout this vast green space. The park provides a quite brilliant splash of life-giving space and colour in the city's mass of brick and concrete. In addition to its architectural jewels and fascinating history, the park is also a refuge for all types of rare plants, insects, birds, fish and animals. The Isblads marsh area, located in the southeastern section of the park, is a popular bird-watching site. The oak trees in the park are hundreds of years old and shelter rare butterflies and beetles. Visit at your own pace: there are excellent footpaths and cycle ways throughout the park.

Explore the archipelago by sea

is an unforgettable experience but bear in mind temperatures can fall to -6°C (21°F) or less. The wind off the water can chill to the bone and there is ice on the surface of the lake even right into the city centre.

POPULATION

Today, half the city is on Lake Mälaren, the other on Saltsjön (Salt Lake), which leads out to the archipelago and the Baltic Sea, and the city continues to grow. From its small beginnings as a trading post and fort, Stockholm had no more than 75,000 inhabitants by the 18th century. At the end of the 19th century, as a result of the late industrial revolution, Swedes flocked by the thousands into the cities. By 1900, Stockholm had 300,000 city-dwellers. Now the population of the inner city stands at 933,000, while the Greater Stockholm region has more than 2.3 million inhabitants.

POLITICS

Sweden is a monarchy but executive power is exercised by the government led by the Prime Minister of Sweden; the monarch now purely a ceremonial and representative figurehead. The Swedish royal family is considered to be 'of the people' and is a popular institution.

The country is a member of the European Union but elected not to adopt the euro in 2003. In 2014 a political crisis emerged when a surge of national-ism was felt from the far right Swedish Democrats, fuelled by anti-immigration sentiment both in political circles and in the country as a whole. The party gained seats for the first time and has proved a force to be reckoned with for Prime Minister Stefan Löfven and his minority government.

ECONOMICS

As life progresses in the third millennium, rapid technical developments and globalisation are sparking new job opportunities and attracting new inhabitants to Stockholm. Today the city's residents are very conscious of their modern image. Swedish pop music has become an international industry that is generating a new sense of confidence. The city also plays a leading international role in information technology and biotechnology. Taking advantage of Stockholmers' reputation for being open-minded, trend-hungry and tech-friendly, fashion houses and IT firms regularly use the city as a testing ground for new products.

This is an affluent city with a high standard of living. Stockholmers live and dress well, and in the shops you will find plenty of the clean, well made no-nonsense designer goods that have put Swedish design on the international map. Visitors, however, may find the prices for eating out and entertainment are high but costs for public transport are reasonable to encourage environmentally friendly travel.

The iconic golden room at Stadhuset

CULTURE AND SOCIAL LIFE

Stockholm is a city of growing cultural and social diversity, where waves of immigration have changed the texture of a once homogenous society. This is reflected in the abundance of ethnic restaurants and the international influence on traditional Swedish cuisine. Yet while they love a good meal, a night at the opera and dancing into the wee hours at trendy night-

DON'T LEAVE STOCKHOLM WITHOUT...

Going for a *fika*. For more than 100 years Swedes have been observing a tradition of relaxing over coffee accompanied by baked goods: to *fika*. Pronounced 'fee-ka', it is widely translated as taking a break *(fikarast)* to socialize over coffee. See page 18.

Tucking into a *smörgåsbord*. The *smörgåsbord* first appeared at Swedish tables in the 18th century. Although not so available these days, it's worth seeking out a restaurant with *smörgåsbord* on the menu to experience this age-old culinary tradition. See page 19.

Exploring the archipelago. A boat trip to the islands is a must in this unique city that owes so much of its charm to nearly 30,000 islands and skerries, where you can enjoy delightful settlements, outdoor activities and nature in abundance. See page 72, 75, 78 and 88.

Seeing the city from the top of the Ericsson Globe. SkyView is a glass gondola ride that takes 20 minutes and offers amazing views from 130m (426ft) above sea level. Reserve a time on the website before visiting to avoid the lines. See page 22.

Browsing an indoor food market. The hustle and bustle of Hörtorgshallen, a colourful food hall filled with enticing delicacies from around the world, is absorbing. Go on a gastronomical journey and you'll also find cafés and restaurants serving up speciality meals and snacks, all under one roof. See page 40.

Seeking out Swedish design. Swedish designers have won worldwide acclaim for their clean lines with an emphasis on natural materials. Keep an eye out for Bruno Mathsson's Pernilla armchair (1942); the remarkable concrete chair (1980s) by Jonas Bohlin; and the work of emerging young glass designer Ann Wåhlström. See page 21.

Admiring royal pageantry. The best way to get a feel for Stockholm's royal family is to watch the daily changing of the guard outside the palace. See page 32

Ambling the narrow streets of Gamla Stan. Discover interesting shops, hidden quaint cafés, top-end restaurants, history and important buildings, all crammed into the shady narrow lanes and courtyards. See page 30.

Going back in time. Be amazed by the warship *Vasa*, at the Vasamuseet, a superb example of a vessel that lay preserved on the ocean floor for 333 years. See page 48.

clubs, even the most sophisticated city-dwellers are happiest when they can swim naked and bond with nature. Much of Stockholm's beauty arises from the fact that only about a third of the city's surface area is concrete and asphalt; the rest is parks and water, and the great outdoors is but a short drive away.

Swedes may at first seem a little cool and formal, but beneath that composed exterior and self-satisfaction with all things Swedish, they are a friendly people – especially after one or two schnapps. The unyielding state monopoly on alcohol has created a sense of deprivation that causes many Swedes to over-indulge when they have the chance. Yet when it comes to dining, proper etiquette is in order, from arriving punctually to the smallest of glances exchanged with other dinner guests before and after the traditional toast, or *skål*.

Children

Few major European cities share Stockholm's reputation for welcoming children. You might be surprised to discover how many amenities and how much entertainment is planned around the needs of the youngest inhabitants and visitors. Many of the city's parks allow children to borrow toys, sporting equipment and bicycles at no charge. Parents with pushchairs benefit from 'kneeling' buses and many other services designed with families in mind.

CONFIDENT CITY

Throughout its rich and varied history the city has shown a remarkable ability to adapt to changing times while creating a vibrancy that is all its own. It could be said that Stockholm never really lost its Viking fervour for the conquest of new worlds. Throughout the city you will see how the old has been fused to the new, often to startling effect.

Of late, Stockholm has rebranded itself the 'capital of Scandinavia', causing hackles to rise in Copenhagen and Oslo. But there are reasons for Stockholm's confidence in its grand claims: it is the largest city in the largest country in Scandinavia, it has the most multinational companies and the largest stock market, and receives the highest number of visitors from around the globe. Stockholm is the powerhouse of Sweden, and accounts for more than one-fifth of the country's employment and a quarter of its total production. Yet this is no noisy, industrial city, and there is space for everyone.

This modern and sophisticated metropolis is also famous for Scandinavian design in furniture, textiles and interiors and plays host to a number of international festivals. Once considered a place of *husmanskost* ('homely fare'), the city now features some of the top chefs and most exciting cuisine in Europe. Stockholm's nightlife has exploded into an array of young, hip

An aerial view over the islands that form the city of Stockholm

clubs and older, more sedate nightspots offering music and ambience for every taste. Infusing the old with the new is a speciality of today's vibrant Stockholm, as quick to seize on a new trend as Milan or Paris.

TOP TIPS FOR EXPLORING STOCKHOLM

The Stockholm Pass. The Stockholm Pass offers the holder free entry to 65 museums, tours and other attractions. Validity is for one (595kr), two (795kr), three (995kr) or five (1,295kr) days. Purchase your card online at www.stockholmpass.com.

Underground art. Take note when travelling on Stockholm's subway. Sometimes referred to as 'the world's longest art gallery', over 90 of the 100 stations have been embellished with exciting art, mosaics, installations and sculptures.

Food on a budget. Discover Stockholm's food trucks (www.stockholmfoodtrucks.nu), rolling restaurants serving a variety of cuisines such as a Vietnamese, Turkish, Mexican, vegetarian and raw foods. Good fast food at a good price!

Night lights. After dark the city lights twinkle against the water. Walk around the coast of Skeppsholmen at night, especially during winter when all the Christmas lights in central Stockholm are lit.

Sales. Twice a year – late June to the end of July and from after Christmas throughout January – the city's shops and department stores have their sales with reduced prices on clothing, shoes and other fashion goods. Watch out for the rea sign if you want to grab a bargain.

Hop-on-hop-off. Getting around a 'city that floats on water' is easy with a hop-on hop-off combination ticket. Boats and buses journey over land and water, and the combination ticket gives you access to 7 boat stops and 25 bus stops (www.redsightseeing.com).

Frozen city. The city is enchanting in the dead of winter when snow makes picture-postcard scenery. But the downfall is that it can get bitterly cold and the waterways often freeze over (allowing Stockholmers to ice skate). Hence a number of boat tours out to the islands do not run during the winter months.

Free walking tours. Friendly tour guides offer two daily free walking tours in English (10am and 1pm), plus two late afternoon free tours at the weekends. There's no need to book, just turn up at the starting point (www.stockholmfreetour.com).

Vintage tram. From April until November Djurgårdslinjen, a voluntary organisation of tram enthusiasts, operate lovingly restored trams between Norrmalmstorg and Djurgården, where 14 vintage trams are stabled at the end of the route. Refreshments are served on some services.

Midsummer. The most important celebration of the year for many Swedes, Midsummer always takes place on a Friday between 19 June and 25 June, when locals celebrate the longest day of the year. This is what materialises from being kept in the dark all winter!

Freshly caught seafood

FOOD AND DRINK

Sweden, once known for its 'husmanskost' (traditional homely fare), is enjoying a culinary renaissance. Swedish chefs love New Nordic cuisine, popularised by Noma in Copenhagen, which focuses on simply-prepared food and fresh, local organic produce.

Stockholm borrows the best from the rest of the country and abroad, making its top-end restaurants a truly exciting gastronomic experience. A variety of ethnic styles of cooking are combined to create surprising and delicious dishes generally referred to as 'crossover' cuisine. But, of course, you can still sample husmanskost and the famous Swedish *smörgåsbord* (see box), albeit nowadays they can be harder to find in Stockholm.

LOCAL CUISINE

The best way to describe the Swedish approach to food is 'natural'. There's a new feeling of joy and experimentation when it comes to the country's natural resources, whether that's reindeer, venison or elk; fish from the rivers, lakes and sea; or mushrooms and berries gathered in the forests and on the tundra of Sweden's far north, where the local Sami culture has a strong influence on the cuisine.

For the true Swedish experience look for restaurants serving *husmanskost*, such as *Janssons frestelse* (a creamy baked dish of shredded potatoes, herring and onion); *pytt i panna* (a fry-up of potatoes, onions, meat and sausage); *dillkött* (lamb or veal in dill sauce); *köttbullar* (meatballs served with tangy lingonberry sauce); *strömming* (fried, boned herring from the Baltic Sea); *färskpotatis* (a dish of new potatoes boiled with dill and served with a pat of butter; and on Thursdays, join almost all locals in eating *ärtsoppa* (yellow-pea and pork soup), followed by *pannkakor med sylt* (pancakes with jam). However, in New Nordic style, these are all often reinvented with a new twist. *Sill* (pickled herring) is an acquired taste but, served with new potatoes, is an essential part of midsummer.

Bounded by the sea and with some 96,000 lakes dotting its countryside, Sweden has an abundant supply of fish, which naturally plays an important role in the country's diet. Salmon is a common ingredient, with less of a luxury connotation than in some other countries. *Gravad lax* (marinated salmon) and *rökt lax* (smoked salmon) are common components of the *smörgåsbord*.

Wild berries and mushrooms are highly prized, especially since food prices are high. Swedish law gives everyone the right, known as *allemansrätten*, to wander through fields and forests to pick

Michelin–rated Oaxen Krog   *Traditional fika*

these gifts of nature. Even city dwellers, never too far away from the great outdoors, take the opportunity to gather *smultron* (wild strawberries), *blåbär* (blueberries), *hjortron* (Arctic cloudberries), *svamp* (mushrooms) and *lingon* (wild cranberries).

The seasons
Each season has traditional specialities and any discussion of eating habits must take these into account. Some regional dishes, such as blood soup and fermented herring, may sound less than appetising, but those visitors with adventurous palates will want to try at least a few of those foods that time-honoured custom prescribe. Summertime means almost 24-hour daylight in Sweden. It's a season when people can luxuriate in fruit and vegetables that have been grown locally under the midnight sun, instead of the expensive imported produce available during much of the year.

Breakfast
A traditional Swedish breakfast *(frukost)* at a café usually consists of a cup of coffee or tea with slices of bread, butter and marmalade, and cheese. Other toppings might include slices of ham or salmon, with maybe some lettuce and tomato. A much more substantial breakfast with eggs, bacon, or ham will certainly be available at your hotel where a breakfast buffet is often included in the price. Also found at breakfast, be sure to try *knäckebröd* (crisp rye bread), which

comes in a wide selection and is something worth taking back home, along with some cheese: there are more than 200 different cheeses to choose from. Look for *vasterbottenost*, *herrgårdsost* and *sveciaost* – these are typical hard, well-aged cheeses.

WHERE TO EAT

Restaurants
Stockholm's restaurant scene has exploded over the last 10 years and is one of the most varied European cities for eating out, although it can be pretty expensive. The city boasts its own superstar chefs with nine glittering Michelin-starred eateries to choose from, including Oaxen Krog, Operäkallaren Matsal and Mathias Dahlgren (see page 98). Alongside these are a host of other modern concept restaurants with innovative kitchens that have garnered successes and offer an elite dining experience. You will also find a multitude of restaurants all over the city that are not quite so prestigious, which still offer an excellent standard of cooking and that will not put so much pressure on the credit card.

Budget options
For travellers on a tight budget there is no shortage of fast-food outlets, pubs, ethnic restaurants, kebab houses, cafeterias and pizzerias, including the ubiquitous *korvkiosk* selling grilled chicken, sausages, hamburgers and *tunnbröds-*

Wild mushroom picking

rulle (a parcel of mashed potato, sausage and ketchup wrapped in soft bread). Some also serve *strömming* (fried herring) and mashed potato. There are hot-dog kiosks located all over the city; this once-American speciality has become a favourite snack of Stockholmers, particularly when the hot dog is served in a soft wrap-around bread called *tunnbröd*, and complemented with a generous dollop of mashed potatoes. Look for the *dagens rätt* (dish of the day), which usually includes a main course, bread, salad and soft drink for a set price. It's also worth investigating the market halls, for example Östermalmshallen (www.ostermalmshallen. se) and Hötorgshallen (see page 40), where you can pick up delicious deli nibbles to make your own picnic.

Vegetarian

You can find some good vegetarian restaurants in Stockholm – in fact they are on the increase as vegetarian and healthy food is becoming more and more popular – and most eateries have a selection of good quality vegetarian dishes on the menu.

Cafés

Stockholm's array of cafés deserves its own special mention, which are particularly appealing when they spread outside onto the streets and squares in summer. Cafés can also be found in department stores, shopping malls and some museums. Going for a *fika* is a very Swedish tradition, involving curling up in a cosy charming café with a steaming cup of coffee and a cinnamon bun with a couple of good friends or family to gossip the morning away. *Fika* is also combined in words such as *fikabröd* (fika bread), which is a collective name for all kinds of biscuits, cookies, buns, etc. that are traditionally eaten with coffee. Non-sweetened breads are normally not included in this term (even though these may sometimes be consumed with coffee).

WHAT TO DRINK

Coffee – which is excellent – is consumed in great quantities at all times of the day and night, and forms a recognised part of Stockholm's social life. Gourmet coffee is a rising trend in the city, with some cafés splashing out on their own roasting equipment. The Swedes also drink a lot of milk with their meals. In addition, yoghurt and other kinds of fermented milk are popular. During colder months, hot chocolate topped off with cream and marshmallows is popular.

Food and Drink Prices

Price guide for an average two-course meal for one with a glass of house wine throughout this book:

$$$$ = over 750 kr
$$$ = 450–750 kr
$$ = 250–450 kr
$ = below 250 kr

Classic Swedish meatballs   *Aquavit on ice*

Alcohol

Teetotaller organisations are a powerful factor in Swedish politics and this has led to very high taxes on alcoholic beverages, especially hard liquor, in order to discourage drinking. Outside restaurants, with the exception of a very weak beer that can be bought in grocery stores or supermarkets, alcohol is sold only by *Systembolaget*, the state-owned liquor monopoly. *Systembolaget* stores, recognisable by a green-and-yellow rectangular sign, stock a vast range of brands of whisky, vodka, gin, and so forth, but wine is by far the best value for your money. The stores usually open Mon–Fri 10am–6pm and Sat until 3pm (see page 112).

Swedes drink more beer than wine. Commercial products tend to be bland lager-style beers, but craft breweries are increasingly popular. Sweden also has some excellent indigenous schnapps, usually drunk with herring. Tap water is safe to drink all over the country.

Sweden's national drink, *aquavit* (or *snaps*), is distilled from potatoes or grain and flavoured with herbs and spices, coming in many varieties. *Aquavit* should always be consumed with food, especially herring; it should be served ice-cold in small glasses, swallowed in a gulp or two and washed down with a beer or mineral water. When you see a bottle with the word LINE on it, you'll know it is special stuff. In the old days, barrels of *aquavit* went with the sailors and they swore that it tasted better after having returned from a voyage that had crossed the equator. These days the custom is continued. Barrels are specially sent to cross the line, and when they return the liquor is bottled and the details of the voyage are detailed on the back of the label, and can be read through the bottle.

Other specialities include *glögg*, a hot, spiced wine at Christmas, and *punsch* (punch), which is usually served after dinner, well-chilled, with coffee.

The smörgåsbord

The *smörgåsbord* can be hard to find sometimes, except on Sunday afternoons and during the Christmas season. Strömma Kanalbolaget's brunch boat tour serves a tasty *smörgåsbord* (tel: 08-120 040 00; www.stromma.se). The *smörgåsbord* table (or groaning board, if you will) can consist of as many as 100 different dishes. It should not be tackled haphazardly. The first thing to remember is not to overload your plate – you can go back for more as many times as you wish. Even more important is the order in which you eat. Start by sampling the innumerable herring dishes, taken with boiled potatoes and bread and butter. Then move on to other seafood, like smoked or boiled salmon, smoked eel, Swedish caviar and shrimp. Next come the delightful egg dishes, cold meats (try the smoked reindeer) and salads. The small warm dishes are next – meatballs, fried sausages and omelettes – and finally, finish with sweets, cheese and fruit.

Bruka Design showcases the best of Swedish furniture and homeware design

SHOPPING

Stockholm is a shopping destination to be reckoned with, no matter where you look – from the big modern exclusive department stores, modern malls and small boutiques to its somewhat bohemian and unique neighbourhood shops.

When it comes to shopping, Stockholm has something for everyone. Here you'll discover the Swedish design that has become famous worldwide for its simplicity and functionality. The majority of the best retail opportunities are clustered in the city centre, with most shops within easy walking distance of each other. From fashion, antiques and handicrafts to local foods and modern interior design, it's all here.

WHERE TO SHOP

For fun shopping in a medieval milieu, try exploring Gamla Stan the place to go for souvenirs, handicrafts and unusual knick-knacks. Västerlånggatan, the pedestrian street bisecting the island, and the lanes surrounding it are lined with shops and boutiques. For more unique shopping head to Södermalm, a young creative neighbourhood with trendy design and clothing shops as well as antiques and second-hand shops, particularly around Götgatan, Hornsgatan and Folkungagatan streets. In the exclusive Östermalm are international labels, including Marc Jacobs and Prada, alongside local talented designers such as Filippa K and Johan Lindeberg. If you're looking for upmarket fashion shops, you should head for the 'golden triangle' bordered by Norrmalmstorg, Nybroplan and Stureplan. Stockholm has preserved a wealth of antiques for sale at reasonable prices and antique lovers should check out the shops on Odengatan, Upplandsgatan and Roslagsgatan.

Department stores and malls

There are two large department stores in the centre. Prestigious Nordiska Kompagniet (see page 40) is Stockholm's majestic store and a city landmark while Åhléns City (Klarabergsgatan 50) is Sweden's largest department store known for its inexpensive, quality homewares and food department.

The two main city-centre malls are the elegant Sturegallerian near Stureplan (www.sturegallerian.se) and the larger and less expensive Gallerian on Hamngatan (www.gallerian.se).

Markets

Just before you leave Stockholm, it is worth making an effort to visit one of the colourful market halls, Hörtorgshallen (see page 40), Östermalmshal-

Culinary treats at Östermalmshallen food market

len (Östermalmstorg) or Soderhallarna (Medborgarplatsen), for Swedish delicacies such as reindeer and elk meat, cloudberries, caviar, fish and cheese specialities, crisp bread and a bottle of aquavit, the throat-burning national drink. Market halls are all closed Sunday and public holidays.

WHAT TO BUY

Design and interior decoration

Shopping in Stockholm is a delightful entry into the world of design – especially on furniture and products for the home – ranging from affordable high-street shops like Hemtex (Sergelgatan 17), to more exclusive stores like Design Torget (Sergels Torg 3) and Svenskt Tenn (Strandvägen 5). Top products include glassware, ceramics, stainless-steel cutlery, silver, furniture and textiles. Sweden's fine reputation in these fields rests on old traditions of skilled craftsmanship passed down through generations. Rörstrand (Stortorget 223) in Gamla Stan is a predominant name in the field of ceramics, but there are many smaller companies. The wide choice ranges from fanciful items that easily fit in your suitcase to one-of-a-kind sculptures with a price tag to match their considerable size. Glassware is one of Sweden's most famous design products. Names such as Orrefors and Kosta Boda are recognised worldwide, and talented artists and artisans working for these and other companies consistently produce inventive designs. Nordiska Kristal is the best for glassware and has a main shop and art gallery downtown at Norrlandsgatan 13.

Souvenirs and handicrafts

Nordic knitwear is everywhere. Kilgren (Våsterlånggatan 45) in Gamla Stan is a long-established shop selling a wide range of Nordic sweaters, Scottish kilts and cashmeres and handmade traditional knives. Also in Gamla Stan, Oleana (Järntorget 83) is a Norwegian company that produces beautifully designed women's sweaters and cardigans. Although Stockholm is a long way from Lapland, many shops sell a range of knife handles, pouches and other goods handcrafted out of reindeer antlers and skins. Silversmiths fashion innovative necklaces, bracelets and rings, as well as stunning silver bowls and cigarette cases. Other typical souvenirs are painted linen tapestries, clogs and handmade dolls. At Tyska brinken in the old town is the whimsical Tomtar & Troll, with the handmade trolls that are at the heart of Swedish folklore. Tomtar are small creatures that, if treated with respect, will protect the household. The Swedes say that every house should have one – just in case.

If you must have a hand-painted red Dalarna horse, named after the province of Dalarna, or any other classic Swedish handicraft, you should take care to shop wisely. For every shop with quality products, there are a dozen with flimsy imitations.

Drottningholms Slottsteater

ENTERTAINMENT

Stockholm's entertainment scene is varied and vibrant, with new venues opening up all the time. Wild clubs, buzzing bars, sedate hotel lounges, live rock, sensational jazz, superb opera and ballet: whatever your taste, the city has it in abundance.

The entertainment possibilities in Stockholm may not be equal to those of, say, New York or London, but it is thriving and will satisfy the desires of any visitor. Most venues are within easy walking distance of each other and the centre so, whether you're enjoying *La Traviata* at the Opera House or some modern jazz at an intimate club in Gamla Stan, you should not have far to go. Moreover, the long, light Stockholm summer nights are made-to-order for relaxing outdoor options. Glance at the listings in a daily newspaper and you'll find multiple choices among pop and rock clubs alone. This is not surprising, given that Swedish music's sometimes significant position on the world stage has made it such an important export item.

MUSIC AND DANCE

Stockholmers are great supporters of classical music, opera and ballet. The massive auditorium of the Konserthuset (see page 106) is the principal venue for music performances during the winter months, the season stretching from September to May or June. In summer you can enjoy concerts in a variety of splendid settings scattered throughout the Stockholm area – Music at the Palace heralds the start of the summer concert season in the Hall of State and the Royal Chapel at the Royal Palace (see page 32). The city's churches give regular concerts, such as the tranquil setting of Jacobs Kyrka (see page 42) and the Storkyrkan (see page 32) in the old town. Opera has been performed in Sweden since 1773, and first-rate productions are offered at Kungliga Operan (see page 106), the Swedish national venue.

This creative city is the birthplace of music phenomena like ABBA and the city attracts music talent from all over the world. An increasing number of venues host live events: check the local press for details of upcoming shows. The Ericsson Globe (www.stockholmlive.com/en/our-arenas/ericsson-globe), just south of the city centre, is a standard stop on the touring schedule of numerous international stars. Stockholm Jazz Festival (www.stockholmjazz.com) brightens the darkening days of October with a 10-day event of public screenings and the presentation of awards.

Kungliga Operan is also where you can see ballet at its best – famous ballets

A summer music festival *Walpurgis Eve at Skansen*

such as *Swan Lake* are performed during the season. Stockholm is also noted for modern dance, and Dansens Hus (see page 106) attracts many established dance companies.

There are also open-air concerts in many of the city parks, including Kungsträdgården (see page 41) in the heart of town. The famous open-air museum of Skansen (see page 49) has a full and varied summer season of outdoor entertainment. This may include anything from a performance by an orchestra to a foreign dance troupe.

THEATRE

Stockholm has a lively theatrical life. However, nearly all performances are in Swedish. Ask at the Stockholm Visitor Centre (see page 114) about shows staged in English, particularly during the summer. In summer the Drottningholm Slottsteater (see page 106) opens its summer season of concerts, operas and dance in the 18th-century court theatre. Modern and classical plays are staged at Sweden's national theatre, Kungliga Dramatiska Teatern (see page 106), and Stockholm Stadsteater (see page 106).

CINEMA

There are many cinemas in the city centre, and virtually all non-Swedish speaking visitors can enjoy a film in their own language. Local newspapers have full details of films and times. Book a ticket in advance through the websites of the two major film companies: sf (www.sf.se) and Sandrews (www.sandrewmetronome.se).

NIGHTLIFE

Nightclubs and discos usually start to get lively at 10 or 11pm and generally close between 3 and 5am. Unfortunately, many nightclubs have long queues outside from 9pm or 10pm, even if they are not full inside. This is an irritating way of showing that the club is popular. Avoid the queues by arriving early, or book a table for dinner so that you don't have to pay the entrance fee. Many have live dance music; some also offer cabaret and variety shows. If you sit at a table you are expected to eat; at the bar ordering food is unnecessary. In addition to nightclubs, there are also dance restaurants in town that close earlier, at around 1am. Note that though the cost of drinking has fallen a little in recent years, a night on the town can still be expensive.

FESTIVALS

This is a city of festivals, where celebrations concentrate on everything from food to art and music. Celebrated in traditional ways in Stockholm, they are highly popular with locals and tourists alike. No matter what time of year you visit the city, you will find an abundance of festivals to keep you entertained. For a full festival and events calendar see www.visitstockholm.com.

Cycling in Djurgården

OUTDOOR ACTIVITIES

Sweden is a health-conscious and outdoor nation, so it's not surprising that the Stockholm region boasts excellent sporting facilities. There are also all kinds of opportunities to get out and enjoy the green spaces throughout the city.

Water sports such as sailing, swimming, water skiing, windsurfing, canoeing and fishing are very popular, as you would expect in a city that virtually floats on water. Swedes are also fond of jogging, hiking and cross-country skiing and there are many trails for these activities in nearby wooded areas. A number of recreational facilities are located in Djurgården, where you can rent a bike, go horse riding and enjoy hiking or just strolling. Visitors who wish to centre their holiday around sport can download information from the Visit Stockholm website (www.visitstockholm.com).

WATERSPORTS

Canoeing. Sweden is well-equipped for canoeists. Visit www.kanotcenter.com for detailed information on locations and canoe hire facilities. The sheltered waters of the Stockholm archipelago are also good for sea kayaking.

Fishing. Pollution has been eliminated from Stockholm's waters over the past few years, and it's now possible to fish for salmon in Strömmen, the stream that flows past the Royal Palace. There is good fishing in Lake Mälaren, in the smaller lakes in the city environs and around the 24,000 islands of the archipelago in the Baltic Sea. A fishing permit is not required in the city, but is elsewhere; it can be purchased online at www.ifiske.se, www.sportfiskarna.se or check with the tourist office.

Sailing. During the summer there are numerous boats on Lake Mälaren, in the archipelago and skimming through the city's waterways. There are at least ten places in the Stockholm area where boats can be rented (check with the tourist office) and special harbours for visitors with their own boats. However, sailing through the labyrinth of islands that make up the Stockholm archipelago is not to be attempted by amateurs. Opportunities for sailing adventures abound, with many charter companies running day cruises or longer, to picturesque islands. Stockholm Adventures operate day sails in a historic schooner luxury yacht (www.stockholm adventures.se).

Swimming. In the Stockholm region there are 200km (125 miles) of beaches – both sea and lake bathing – including several at Riddarfjärden, near the city centre. On the outskirts of Södermalm is one of the biggest swimming complexes

Kayaking on the archipelago

Stockholm's ski slope

Eriksdalsbadet (www.eriksdalsbadet.se) including two outdoor pools for the summer months. One of the most pleasant outdoor pools is Vanadisbadet, near Sveavägen (May–mid-Sept).

Windsurfing. The surf centre (www.vindsurfing.se) can be found right in the centre of the city at Rålambshovsparken in the Kungholmen district. The minimum age is 13 years.

WINTER SPORTS

Skating. The most popular and conspicuous outdoor rink is in Kungsträdgården (in the centre of town). However, many Swedes prefer long-distance skating along the frozen waterways of Lake Mälaren and the Baltic Sea in winter, when the ice is thick enough. Skates can be hired from most popular locations. You can also hire a guide in Stockholm to take you out on the city's frozen canals in January and early February: Stockholm ICEguide (www.iceguide.se).

Skiing. Easily reached by public transport (10 minutes) the city ski resort of Hammarbybacken (www.skistar.com/hammarbybacken) is the closest option for a spot of skiing. Being on a man-made hill is reliant on a good cold snap for the best conditions.

MORE ACTIVITIES

Cycling. There are plenty of opportunities to cycle in and around Stockholm; www.visitstockholm.com gives information.

Djurgården is particularly good for safe cycling with graded cycle tracks; bikes can be hired from Djurgårdsbrons Sjö-café (www.sjocafet.se). City Bikes (see page 117) provide bikes for hire at docking stations around the city.

Golf. Golf is a popular summertime activity. In the Stockholm area the following golf courses stand out: Djursholms Golfklubb (www.dgk.nu) and Saltsjöbadens Golfklubb (www.saltsjobadengk.se).

Hiking. There are plenty of easy, marked walking trails, which start just outside Stockholm. The summer trails are indicated by raised or painted stones and all-season trails by crosses. There are day-long or longer trails and you can reach most starting points by bus from the city centre. The three major hiking trails are Sörmlandsleden, Upplandsleden and Roslagsleden; the tourist office has further information.

Horse riding. Ride in Djurgården with Häståikeriet (www.hastakeriet.se). Beginners and experienced riders are catered for; one-hour, two-hour and day rides are available.

Hot-air ballooning. Experience the city from above (see page 114).

Rooftop walking. Take a rooftop tour (www.takvandring.com). A combination of climbing and sightseeing, safety is of primary concern and equipment is provided. Not for those with vertigo.

Tennis. Two of the best venues, with indoor and outdoor courts, are Tennisstadion (www.tennisstadion.se); and Kungliga Tennishallen (www.kltk.se).

A line drawing of Stockholm, depicted in 1693

HISTORY: KEY DATES

Stockholm owes its existence to its natural waterways, ideal for trade. Its strong central government helped to create a world power whilst a golden age of cultural advancement made a liberal, forward-thinking nation, with Stockholm at its centre.

EARLY YEARS

1252	Stockholm is first mentioned in a letter by its founder Birger Jarl.
1397	Kalmar Union links the Nordic countries.
1471	Sten Sture the Elder defeats the Danish King Kristian at Brunkeberg.
1520	Swedish noblemen executed in the notorious Stockholm Bloodbath.

THE VASA ERA

1523	Gustav Vasa, the newly appointed king, marches into Stockholm.
1527	Parliament confiscates Church property during the Reformation.
1560	Gustav Vasa dies.
1561	Erik XIV is crowned king and curbs the power of his brothers, who later imprison him at Gripsholms Slott; he dies in 1577, probably poisoned.
1569	Johan III crowned in Stockholm.
1611	Gustav II Adolf comes to power.
1618	The Thirty Years' War starts in Germany.
1632	Gustav II Adolf killed in battle at Lutzen.
1633	Six-year-old Kristina becomes queen; guardians rule the country.
1654	Kristina abdicates and Karl X Gustav is crowned king.
1697	Tre Kronor Castle destroyed by fire; Karl XII, aged 15, is crowned.
1719	New constitution transfers power from the king to parliament.

THE GOLDEN AGE

1741	Botanist Carl von Linné appointed professor at Uppsala.
1772	The new king, Gustav III, orchestrates a bloodless *coup d'état* that gives the king absolute power.
1786	Swedish Academy founded.
1792	Gustav III murdered.

Nobel Prize Award Ceremony

1809	Sweden loses Finland; Gustav IV Adolf abdicates.
1810	Parliament chooses Jean-Baptiste Bernadotte as Crown Prince.
1814	Sweden gains Norway in peace with Denmark.
1818	Karl XIV Johan crowned king of Sweden and Norway.
1869	Emigration to North America increases due to crop failures.
1876	L M Eriksson starts the manufacture of telephones.
1895	Alfred Nobel establishes the Nobel Prize.

20TH CENTURY

1905	Parliament dissolves the union with Norway.
1921	Universal suffrage introduced.
1939	Sweden's coalition government declares neutrality in World War II.
1940	Swedish–German agreement to allow the transit of German military personnel.
1950	First public TV broadcast in Sweden; Stockholm's first underground railway is inaugurated.
1955	Obligatory national health insurance established.
1973	Gustav VI Adolf dies and is succeeded by his grandson, Carl XIV Gustaf.
1974	The monarch loses all political powers.
1986	Prime Minister Olof Palme is murdered in Stockholm.
1995	Sweden joins the European Union after a referendum.

A NEW MILLENNIUM

2000	Church separates from the state after 400 years.
2003	Foreign Minister Anna Lindh murdered in Stockholm.
2006	Centre-right alliance headed by the Moderate Party wins election.
2009	Church of Sweden says yes to gay marriage.
2010	The Swedish Democrats gain parliamentary seats for the first time.
2012	Princess Victoria gives birth to Estelle, second in line to the throne.
2013	In May a week of suburban racial riots is blamed on social segregation.
2014	Newly elected Prime Minister Stefan Löfven forms a minority government consisting of the Social Democrats and the Greens.
2017	Work is underway on the 12-billion kronor New Slussen project to create a new dynamic urban quarter. 7 April: a terrorist driving a truck ploughs into Ahlens City department store on Drottninggatan, killing 4 people and injuring 15.

BEST ROUTES

A summer's day on Gamla Stan

GAMLA STAN

This route wends its way through the city's oldest quarters, including a stroll past the graceful palaces on Helgeandsholmen, to the heart of the ancient city in Gamla Stan, ending with the serene and sparsely populated island of Riddarholmen.

DISTANCE: 4km (2.5 miles)
TIME: A full day
START: Stadshuset
END: Riddarholmen
POINTS TO NOTE: You can get to Stadshuset by taking the subway to T-Rådhuset or buses 3 and 62. Bear in mind that the building can only be viewed with a guide so start with the 10am tour.

The high island rising between the waters of the Baltic Sea and Lake Mälaren is known as Gamla Stan – the Old Town – one of the largest and best preserved medieval centres in Europe. It is the most visited area by tourists in Stockholm, full of museums, churches and notable buildings, as well as offering excellent restaurants and good shopping.

STADSHUSET

From any part of Stockholm south of Lake Mälaren, **Stadshuset ❶** (City Hall; www.stockholm.se/cityhall; guided tours only daily on the hour from 10am–

3pm, with exceptions Dec–Jan; tower: May–Sept daily 9am–4pm) dominates the skyline.

On the Riddarfjärden water's edge, this is the masterwork of architect Ragnar Östberg. A massive, square, 105m (345ft) tower rises from one corner of an elegant central building constructed with decorated brickwork and with an open-fronted portico facing the lake. The building is topped with spires, domes and minarets, and the roofs are clad in a delicate green copper. Above it gleam the **Tre Kronor**, the three golden crowns that symbolise the country. Östberg began work in 1911 and devoted the next 12 years to Stadshuset. He used 8 million bricks and 19 million gilded mosaic tiles, the latter mostly in the famous Golden Hall. In the gardens of the southern terrace is a statue of Engelbrekt Engelbrektsson, the 15th-century Swedish patriot who championed the cause of the peasants in his native Dalarna.

You can climb the tower for a great view of the city. A procession depicting the figures of St George and the Dragon

Stadshuset   *Stadshuset interior*

emerges twice a day as the bells play a medieval tune.

GOVERNMENT BUILDINGS

Leaving Stadshuset, head east past Stadshusbron to the pedestrian walkway along Klara Mälarstrand and then up the steps to Strömgatan, leading to Riksbron. To your right is the imposing **Riksdagshuset** ❷, the House of Par-

liament, and to your left is **Rosenbad** ('rose bath'), a series of palatial buildings overlooking the Strömmen channel that, since 1981, have housed the Swedish government and the prime minister's private office.

The Jugendstil (Art Nouveau) pink sandstone house on the corner of Fredsgatan and Drottningatan, designed by leading late 19th-century architects, houses the Skåne bank. The Venetian-

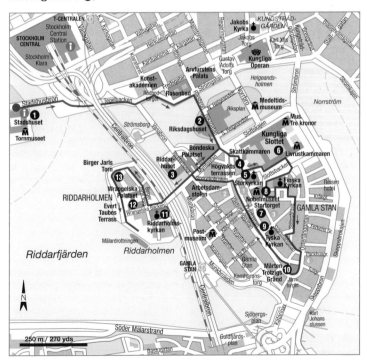

Royal guard

style palace along Strömgatan, the last to be finished (in 1904), was the site of a bank, flats and a restaurant. Rosenbad took its name from a 17th-century bathhouse that offered lily, camomile and rose baths.

Continue south along Riksgatan to Stallbron, leading to Mynttorget, and then turn right to reach **Riddarhuset ❸** (House of Nobility; www.riddarhuset.se; Mon–Fri 11am–noon), one of four parliamentary estates. This is arguably the most beautiful building in Gamla Stan, with two pavilions looking out across the water. Inside, the erstwhile power of the nobles is reflected by the grandeur of the Main Chamber, where the nobles deliberated under the watchful eye of 'Mother Svea', who symbolises Sweden, painted on the ceiling.

CHANGING OF THE GUARD

Leaving Riddarhuset, turn left towards the Kungliga Slottet (Royal Palace), returning to cross Mynttorget and climb up the steps to reach **Högvaktsterassen ❹** where the Royal **Changing of the Guard** (www.forsvarsmakten.se; May–Aug Mon–Sat 12.15pm, Sun and hols 1.15pm, Sept–Mar Wed and Sat 12.15pm, Sun 1.15pm) takes place. This is one of Stockholm's most popular tourist attractions, so arrive early for a good view. Bear right out of the square, cross the road and keeping the cathedral to your left, a good choice for lunch is **Café Sten Sture**, see ❶, at

Trångsund 10, housed in a medieval cellar. If you would rather sit outside, there are several cafés and restaurants in Stortorget.

STORKYRKAN

After lunch, head back along Trångsund to **Storkyrkan ❺** (Great Church; daily 10am–4pm, until 5pm Mon–Fri in summer). This awesome Gothic cathedral is the oldest building in Gamla Stan, part of it dating back to the 12th century. It has high vaulted arches and sturdy pillars stripped back to their original red brick, and a magnificent organ. Storkyrkan's most famous statue, *St George and the Dragon*, a wooden affair carved by Bernt Notke in 1489, is the largest medieval monument in Scandinavia. Check out the 17th-century candelabra and the plaque honouring the three generations of the Tessin family, who built the Royal Palace.

THE ROYAL PALACE

Walk back round the cathedral to Slottsbacken, where you can see a statue of Olaus Petri, the father of the Swedish Reformation. The entrance to the **Kungliga Slottet ❻** (Royal Palace; www.kungahuset.se; May–June, 1–mid Sept daily 10am–5pm, July–Aug 9am–5pm, mid-Sept–Apr Tue–Sun noon–4pm, with exceptions) is on Slottsbacken. The palace, built on the site of the Tre Kronor Palace (which burned down in 1697)

Kungliga Slottet

Ornate tapestries

has 608 rooms, and some of the suites are open to the public. The oldest interiors, dating from the 1660s, are in the north wing. The palace is famous for its tapestries, both of Gobelins and Swedish design. It is still the official residence of the monarch, although the present king, Carl XVI Gustaf, chose to reside at Drottningholm (see page 64). The most evocative room is Oskar II's Writing Room, which has been kept exactly as the king left it when he died in 1907; even his desk is untouched. It is a comfortable, pleasant room, full of 19th-century clutter and family photographs. Be sure not to miss the beautifully preserved rococo interior of the **Royal Chapel** and Queen Kristina's silver throne in the **Hall of State**.

More Royal Palace gems

The **Skattkammaren** (Treasury) beneath the palace holds the stunning Crown Jewels. Immensely valuable and brilliantly lit, they glow in the dim light of the vaults. Also underground is the **Livrustkammaren** (Royal Armoury), which has the stuffed remains of the horse of Gustav II Adolf, who extended Sweden's domain as far as Poland before his death on the battlefield of Lutzen in 1632. The palace is also the site of Gustav III's museum of antiquities (summer only), whose ancient marble sculptures were acquired on the king's journey to Italy, and the **Museum Tre Kronor** in the north wing, which depicts the palace before the 1697 fire.

STORTORGET

Storkyrkan interior

Leaving the Royal Palace by the south entrance turn right into Slottsbacken. At the end of this street turn left, and with the rear of the cathedral to your right continue on into Källargränd, which leads into **Stortorget** ⑦, the central square, with narrow streets fanning out in all directions. Today Stortorget is peaceful, but in medieval times it was a crowded, noisy trading centre where German merchants, stallholders, craftsmen and young servant girls and boys jostled and shouted. Along one side is the old Stock Exchange (Börsen), now home to the **Nobelmuseet** ❽ (The Nobel Museum; www.nobelmuseum. se; July–Aug daily 9am–8pm, Sep–

Soak up the culture in the academic surroundings of Bistro Nobel

May Tue 11am–8pm, Wed–Fri 11am–5pm, Sat–Sun 10am–6pm; guided tours in English available). Using cutting-edge design and technology, including a series of fascinating short films, the museum aims to stimulate interest in culture and the natural sciences; and to document the history and world of the Nobel Prize – specifically the Swedish inventor Alfred Nobel (1833–96) himself and the 800-plus laureates.

Alfred Nobel

Alfred Nobel (1833–96) became a first-rate chemist while still in his teens. Inventor, engineer and industrialist, he held a total of 355 patents during his lifetime. A pacifist at heart, he invented dynamite, which proved a boon to modern warfare; he also patented gelatin and invented smokeless gunpowder. These products formed the basis of his industrial empire, which spread across five continents. Alfred Nobel established the Nobel prizes in his will, drawn up a year before his death. These were for physics and chemistry, for physiological and medical works, for literature and for champions of peace. First awarded in 1901, the prizes for the first four categories have been given at the Nobel Dinner held at Stockholm's Stadshuset (City Hall) on 10th December each year. Nobel directed that the Peace prize be awarded in Oslo, which at his death, and until 1905, was part of Sweden.

Some of the world's most important discoveries and ideas have come from Nobel Prize winners with advances in all aspects of science and medicine, not forgetting the importance of prizes for Peace and Literature. **Bistro Nobel**, see ➋, located in the museum is modelled on the Café Museum in Vienna and is a good place to take a coffee break or lunch.

Site of the Stockholm Bloodbath

As people relax on benches or enjoy a meal at one of the outdoor cafés in the cobbled square, it is hard to imagine that in 1520 it ran with blood during the Stockholm Bloodbath, when the Danish King Kristian II murdered 82 people – not only influential noblemen but any civilian unlucky enough to have a shop or a business nearby. In 1523, after taking revenge against Denmark, Sweden's first heroic king, Gustav Vasa, marched into Stockholm.

AROUND GAMLA STAN

East of Stortorget walk down **Köpmangatan**, which in medieval times was the city's main street. Stop at No. 11, which still has part of its medieval wall intact (although it has the year 1730 inscribed above the doorway). The portal, with its cherubs and a carved hand holding roses, dates back to the beginning of the 17th century. If you peek in through the glass squares of the doorway you will see a medieval passageway leading

The lively shopping street of Västerlånggtan

to a leafy garden that is open in summer – part of an effort in the 1930s to let more light, air and sun into these closely packed houses.

The smallest statue

Retrace your steps on Köpmangatan and turn right onto Trädgårdstvärgrand, which leads to the **Finska Kyrka** (Finnish Church) opposite the palace gate. Behind it is **Bollhustäppan** (Ball Court Garden). This little courtyard has flowers, a small fountain, benches and Stockholm's smallest statue, a figure of a seated boy just 14cm (5.5ins) high. From here, walk down Trädgårdsgatan to Skeppar Olofs Gränd and cross Köpmansgatan to Själargärdsgatan, where you will come to the tree-lined square of **Brända Tomten**, named after a house destroyed in a fire. This prompted the

Nobel Museum

city architect to create in its place a much-needed turning zone for fire engines and other vehicles.

Tyska Kyrkan

Turn right onto Tyska Skolgränd (German School Lane). Together with Tyska Kyrkan (German Church) and Tyska Brinken (German Slope), the lane is a reminder of Germany's overwhelming influence over Stockholm during the 18th century, when the Hanseatic League controlled the Baltic and its ports. The **Tyska Kyrkan** ❾ church on the corner of Svartmangatan and Kindstugatan was founded in 1571 and built in German late-Renaissance and baroque style. Its ebony and alabaster pulpit is unique in Sweden. The altar, dating to the 1640s, is covered with beautiful paintings and is surrounded by sculptures of the evangelists and apostles. If you fancy a change from Swedish food continue a little further north up Svartmangatan to No. 11 where you will find **Texas Longhorn**, see ❸, a definite stop for keen meat-eaters.

Streets of Gamla Stan

Walk back down Svartmangatan to the corner of Baggensgatan (which is named after Admiral Jakob Bagge, 1502–77). Before long you will reach **Österlånggatan** which, together with **Västerlånggatan**, used to constitute a ring around the old city wall. The pedestrian-only Västerlånggtan – lined with tourist shops of every description, bars and restaurants

The peaceful island of Riddarholmen, home to Riddarholmen church

– is very popular and often very crowded, while Österlånggatan, despite being dotted with art galleries, craftsmen's shops and some fine restaurants, is noticeably more tranquil. Look out for **Den Gyldene Freden**, see ❹, a restaurant with a long tradition, at No. 51. It dates from 1722 and was frequented by Swedish troubadour Carl Michael Bellman. The house and restaurant were donated by the Swedish painter Anders Zorn to the Swedish Academy in 1919. This is also a popular choice for dinner later in the evening. The kitchen serves excellent Swedish/French cuisine as well as more modestly priced Swedish home cooking.

Turn right into Järntorget, which is graced by an amusing statue of Evert Taube (1890–1976), the much-loved popular musician, then cross the square into Västerlånggatan and it is a short walk to **Mårten Trotzigs Gränd** ❿ on the left, which at less than a metre wide is the narrowest street in Gamla Stan. Climb up the 36 steps to see how different parts of Gamla Stan vary in height, and how tightly the houses are packed together. At the top turn left on Prästgatan, a quiet, serene street – in stark contrast to the crowded Västerlånggatan, which runs parallel. Note No. 78 with its baroque portal dating from 1670 and rococo doors from the 1750s. Painter Carl Larsson was born here in 1853.

Continuing north up Prästgatan turn left at Storkyrkobrinken until you reach Riddarhustorget. Next to Riddarhu-

set you'll see **Bondeska Palatset** (the Bonde Palace) at No. 8, the seat of the Supreme Court since 1949, created by architect Nicodemus Tessin the Elder in the style of a French town house.

RIDDARHOLMEN

Cross Riddarholmsbron to the quiet island of **Riddarholmen**. On the left is **Riddarholmskyrkan** ⓫, the place for royal burials (Riddarholmen Church; www.kungahuset.se; daily mid-May–mid-Sept 10am–5pm, mid-Sept–Nov Sat–Sun 10am–4pm). The interior is full of ornate sarcophagi, worn gravestones and, in front of the altar, the tombs of the medieval kings Karl Knutsson and Magnus Ladulås. It is built on the site of the late 13th-century Greyfriars Abbey. The vaults contain the remains of all the Swedish monarchs from Gustav II Adolf in the 17th century, with the exception of Queen Kristina, who is buried at St Peter's, Rome, and Gustav VI Adolf, interred at Haga Slott (Haga Castle).

Riddarholmen palaces

Riddarholmen was once the site of many noblemen's residences. At Birger Jarls Torg 4 is Stenbockska Palatset, the best-preserved nobleman's home on Riddarholmen. It was built in the 1640s by the State Councillor Fredrik Stenbock and the family's coat of arms is visible above the porch. In 1969–71 it was restored as the headquarters of the Supreme Court. Across the road is the

The imposing architecture of City Hall as viewed from Evert Taubes Terras

16th-century **Wrangelska Palatset** 🔟 at Birger Jarls Torg 16. The palace was owned by Carl Gustaf Wrangel, a field marshal in the Thirty Years War, and occupied by the royal family after Tre Kronor Castle burned down. The Court of Appeal now occupies the entire building. Continue north to the defensive **Birger Jarls Torn** 🔟 (Birger Jarls Tower) at Norra Riddarholmshamnen. All these buildings are closed to the public.

Walk south towards Riddarfjärden for a fine view across the water from **Evert Taubes Terras**, with Christer Berg's *Solbåten* (Sun Boat) close by, a graceful granite sculpture that resembles a sail. If you fancy an early dinner or a cocktail or return another evening, walk a few steps to *Mälardrottningen*, the yacht once owned by American heiress Barbara Hutton, now a hotel and restaurant (see page 99).

Food and Drink

🔴 CAFÉ STEN STURE

Trångsund 10; tel: 08-20 06 50; www.cafestensture.se; daily 10am– 9pm; $
One for a chilly day, this cellar café oozes character and medieval charm. There's plenty of wholesome mains such as meatballs and steak, plus a range of salads, desserts, cakes and pastries. The set lunch is good value.

🔴 BISTRO NOBEL

Stortorget 2; tel: 08-534 818 12; www.nobelmuseum.se; open as museum hours; $
Drop into this attractive café, decorated in the Viennese style, for a special value lunch or coffee break. Lunch mains may include steamed cod with baked cauliflower or soy braised pork belly. Of course, try the popular Nobel Ice Cream for dessert.

🔴 TEXAS LONGHORN

Svartmangatan 11; tel: 08-20 71 40; www.texaslonghorn.se; Mon–Thu 11am–9.30pm, Fri–Sat 11am–10.30pm Sun noon–9pm; $$
Carnivores rejoice – this place is made for you. On the menu you'll find Texas burgers, rib-eye steak, barbecue ribs and all manner of grills. Vegetarians are not forgotten though with some choice salads and non-meat fajitas. Plenty of dips and sides, and desserts to follow.

🔴 DEN GYLDENE FREDEN

Österlånggatan 51; tel: 08-24 97 60; www.gyldenefreden.se; Mon–Fri 11.30am– 10pm, Sat 1–10pm; $$$
Stockholm's most prestigious restaurant, opened in 1772, was named the 'Golden Peace' after the peace treaty with Russia in 1721. Here you'll find Nordic cooking with a twist, superb service, and an original atmosphere. The special lunch 'dish of the day' is good value.

The lights of the busy commercial district, Sergels Torg

MODERN CITY CENTRE

This district, centred round the New Stockholm or Norrmalm, is the commercial heart of the city where business, banking, shopping and entertainment are concentrated together, along with some serious cultural institutions.

DISTANCE: 2.5km (1.5 miles)
TIME: 2–3 hours
START: Dansmuseet
END: Hamngatan
POINTS TO NOTE: This walk can be combined with Route 3 (see page 41) to take in the lovely Kungsträdgården park just to the east.

In the post-war renewal between the 1950s and the early 1970s, central Stockholm was almost entirely rebuilt and old streets were controversially replaced by office blocks and modern shopping malls with restaurants, cinemas and boutiques. It is now popular with the young and its department stores, chain stores, bars and nightspots are the real draw. It's also a hub of culture for all ages. Many of the buildings are undergoing renovation in an attempt to give the area a 21st-century makeover.

DANSMUSEET

If you are coming from Kungsträdgården metro, walk south down Regeringsgatan and turn right into Jakobsgatan. Take the second right into Drottninggatan. Here at No. 17 happy feet will enjoy a visit to the **Dansmuseet ❶** (www.dansmuseet.se; Tue–Fri 11am–5pm, Sat–Sun noon–4pm; free), a museum dedicated to dance and movement. On display here is the impressive collection of Rolf de Maré (1888–1964), with costumes, masks and photographs on the theme of dance from around the world. Art collector Rolf de Maré was also leader of the Ballets Suédois (Swedish Ballet) in Paris in 1920–25. In 1933 he founded the world's first museum for dance in Paris.

SERGELS TORG

From the museum make your way up Drottninggatan until you come to the main square, **Sergels Torg ❷**, the focal point of the modern city and the main public transport hub. It is the centre of the city's shopping district with traffic circling around a huge glass obelisk that sits in the centre of a fountain, and an open-air pedestrian precinct on the lower level.

Enjoy shopping with the locals on Hamngatan

Kulturhuset

The dominant building in the square is the glass-fronted **Kulturhuset** ❸ (Culture Centre; www.kulturhuset.stockholm.se; Mon–Fri 9am–7pm, Sat–Sun 11am–5pm, with exceptions) where hundreds

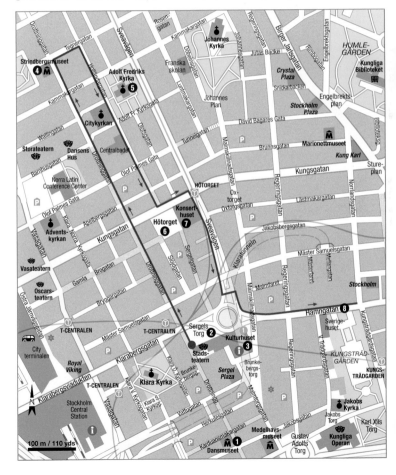

Hotorget, the Concert Hall and the outdoor market in Stockholm's city centre

of people come daily to see art and craft exhibitions, watch films, listen to music or enjoy a fine view of the city while drinking coffee at the **Café Panorama**, see ❶. The **Stockholm Visitor Centre** and the **Stockholm Stadsteater** (Municipal Theatre), which stages modern and classical plays in Swedish, are also located here.

NORTH OF THE CITY CENTRE

Leave the square back on Drottninggatan heading north up the hill and you will find the **Strindbergsmuseet** ❹ (Strindberg Museum; www.strindbergsmuseet.se; Tue–Sun noon–4pm), at Drottninggatan 85, housed in the top-storey flat of the Blåtornet (Blue Tower), where Sweden's greatest playwright spent his last years and wrote his last epic play, *The Great Highway* (1908).

From the museum walk east along Tegnérgatan and take the first right down Holländargatan passing the fine **Adolf Fredriks Kyrka** ❺ (Adolf Fredriks Church; www.adolffredrik.se; Tue–Sun 10am–4pm, Mon 1–6pm) on your left, built between 1768 and 1774.

HÖTORGET

Walking south, crossing the shopping street of Kungsgatan, is **Hötorget** ❻ (Haymarket Square) with a traditional open-air market selling fresh fruit, vegetables and flowers (Mon–Sat; flea market Sun). Check out the newly refurbished **Hörtorgshallen** food hall, with produce to buy and lots of cafés and restaurants.

Also in the square is the **Konserthuset** ❼ (Concert Hall), a neoclassical building with an unusual façade of Corinthian pillars and bronze portals. The Stockholm Philharmonic Orchestra performs here as well as other genres of music. In front of the building you will see Carl Milles' **Orpheus Fountain**, one of the late sculptor's finest works (see page 70).

HAMNGATAN

Make your way south down Sveavägen back to Sergels Torg and take a left into **Hamngatan** ❽, one of the main shopping streets featuring the famous **NK** (Nordiska Kompaniet) department store and Gallerian, a mall with many shops and restaurants. From here you can continue for a well-earned relax in the **Kungsträdgården** (see route 3).

Food and Drink

❶ CAFÉ PANORAMA

Kulturhuset, Sergels Torg 3; tel: 08-21 10 35; www.kulturhusetstadsteatern.se; Mon–Fri 10am–7pm, Sat 10am–6pm, Sun 10am–5pm; $

With good views from the fifth floor of the Kulturhuset, you can get a coffee or a set-menu lunch. There is soup to start with and then a choice of a meat or fish main, such as roast pork loin with pepper sauce or herb baked fish bordelaise.

Beautiful cherry blossom trees line Kungsträdgården in the spring

BLASIEHOLMEN AND SKEPPSHOLMEN

Flanked to the north by Kungsträdgården and an elegant square that is home to the Opera House, the 'museum' islands of Blasieholmen and Skeppsholmen enable you to steep yourself in Scandinavian art, architecture and design.

DISTANCE: 2.5km (1.5 miles)
TIME: Half a day
START: Kungsträdgården
END: Östasiatiska Museet
POINTS TO NOTE: If you are staying in central Stockholm, it's an easy walk to Kungsträdgården, which is opposite the big NK department store on Hamngatan. You can also take the underground to T-Kungsträdgården.

This route provides a complete contrast from the hectic bustle of the city centre and has long been the perfect escape for Stockholmers, both royal and commoners. Blasieholmen features elegant palaces of the 17th and 18th centuries and buildings such as the Nationalmuseum, built in the 19th century. Skeppsholmen's buildings are leftovers from the days when the island was a naval base, bar the striking and resolutely 21st-century Moderna Museet, where you can browse the permanent collection for free.

KUNGSTRÄDGÅRDEN

For centuries, **Kungsträdgården** ❶ has been the city's most popular meeting place and recreational hub. Locals and tourists alike stroll among the lime trees and gather for the many festivals and concerts on the large outdoor stage. In winter, the central skating rink is popular with both children and adults. The king's kitchen garden was located here in the 15th century – this is the city's oldest park. Later Queen Kristina had a stone summer house built here – you can see this lovely 17th-century edifice at Västra Trädgårdsgatan 2 by the cobblestoned Lantmäteribacken.

Encircled by avenues, the Strömgatan end of the park leads to **Karl XIIs Torg**, with J P Molin's statue of the warrior king, sculpted in 1868. Closer to the centre of the park is a statue of Karl XIII (1809–18) by Erik Göthe. Once at the park, you can get coffee at one of any number of cafés along the Kungsträdgårdsgatan side of the park; **Café Söderberg**, see ❶, at the Strömbron end has outdoor tables and a pleasant view.

JAKOBS TORG

Walk to your right through Jakobs Torg, past the 16th-century **Jakobs Kyrka**, dedicated to St Jacob, the patron saint of wayfarers. This leads to **Gustav Adolfs Torg**. The centre of the square features a statue of Gustav II Adolf. On the northeast side is the **Kungliga**

Operan ❷ (Royal Opera House; see page 106), first built in 1782 by Gustav III. In 1792, he was murdered during a masked ball at Operan. In the late 19th century, Axel Anderberg was commissioned to design a new opera house when the old building became a fire hazard. The façade is in late-Renaissance style. In summer, operas

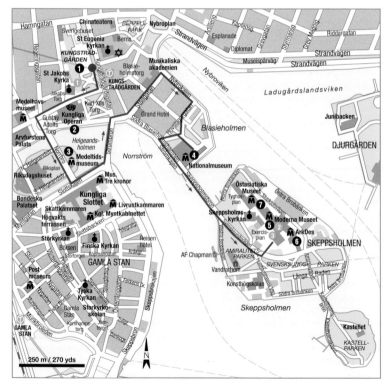

The Royal Opera House, Jakobs Kyrka and the statue of Gustav II Adolf at Jakobs Torg

are performed at Drottningholm (see page 64), but the rest of the year you can enjoy an opera in this regal setting.

On the southwest side of the square is **Arvfurstens Palats** (Prince's Palace), which in 1906 was taken over by the Swedish Foreign Office. It was built for Gustav II's sister, Sofia Albertina, and inaugurated in 1794.

MEDELTIDSMUSEET

Proceed from the centre of the square southeast across Norrbro, which has the Riksdag (Parliament) on one side and, if you follow the steps down on the east side, the **Medeltidsmuseet ❸** (Medieval Museum; www.medeltidsmuseet.stock holm.se; Tue–Sun noon–5pm, Wed until 8pm; free), an underground museum

Cloister garden in the Medeltidsmuseet

built around the capital's archaeological remains. Archaeological digging in the late 1970s revealed part of a city wall dating back to the 1530s. The discovery fortunately put a stop to plans to build a car park on the site. Exhibits include 55m (180ft) of the original town wall, a medieval graveyard and a warship from the 1520s. You can explore reconstructed warehouses and workshops and medieval society is brought to life in a market place, cloister garden and church.

BLASIEHOLMEN

Continue towards the Royal Palace and turn left across Slottskajen then left again onto Strömbron and into **Blasieholmen**. At the traffic lights turn right onto Strömkajen, where sightseeing boats depart for the city as well as the archipelago. You can walk to admire the front of the **Grand Hotel** then backtrack a few metres/yards to go down Stallgatan to **Blasieholmstorg**, where two of the city's oldest palaces are separated by two bronze horses. The palace at No. 8 was originally built in the mid-17th century, and then rebuilt 100 years later in the style of an 18th-century French palace. It used to host foreign ambassadors and is now known as Utrikesministerhotellet (Foreign Ministry Hotel). The offices of the Musical Academy and Swedish Institute are here. Bååtska Palatset stands nearby at No. 6. The newly restored exterior dates from 1699, when it was designed by Tessin the Elder. It

was partly rebuilt in 1876 for the Free-masons, who still have their lodge here.

Nationalmuseum

At the end of the square, at No. 10, note the façade facing onto Nybroka-jen, a handsome example of the neo-Renaissance style of the 1870s and 1880s. Take a right to Nybrokajen and right again to Hovslagaregatan, to go through Musieparken to the entrance of the **Nationalmuseum** ❹ (National Museum of Fine Arts; www.national museum.se; under restoration, due to open in 2018). The building, designed in Venetian and Renaissance styles and completed in 1866, houses Sweden's largest art collection, with 16,000 paint-ings, sculptures, decorative artworks, drawings and prints from the 15th to the early 20th centuries. One of the world's

Carl Larson painting, Nationalmuseum.

oldest museums, the collection includes works by Rembrandt, El Greco, Rubens, Goya, Gauguin, Renoir, Manet and many more. While the museum is closed tem-porary exhibitions of works can be found throughout the city.

SKEPPSHOLMEN

The narrow stretch of water between Bla-sieholmen and **Skeppsholmen** is sur-mounted by a small wrought-iron bridge, Skeppsholmsbron. From the bridge there are magnificent views across to Strandvägen. Moored off the shore near here is the 100-year-old *af Chapman* (see page 96), the sleek schooner that has been given a new lease of life as a youth hostel. Continuing along the road is the **Moderna Museet** ❺ (Mod-ern Museum; www.modernamuseet.se; Tue, Fri 10am–8pm, Wed–Thu 10am–6pm, Sat–Sun 11am–5pm; free). With more than 5,000 paintings, sculp-tures, 25,000 watercolours, drawings and around 100,000 photographs, the museum's collection of 20th-century international and Swedish art is consid-ered one of the finest in the world. There is also a fabulous **restaurant**, see ❷, and espresso bar, which has a terrace and amazing waterside views from its floor-to-ceiling windows.

ArkDes

The **ArkDes** ❻ (Swedish Centre for Archi-tecture and Design; www.arkdes.se; times as Moderna Museet; free; audio

Panoramic views of the leafy islands of Skeppsholmen and Kastellholmen from Södermalm

guide available), shares the entrance and restaurant with the Moderna Museet. The collection guides visitors through 1,000 years of Scandinavian architecture, from the simplest wooden houses to state-of-the-art techniques and styles. There are models of architectural works world-wide, from 2000BC to the present day. The museum's archive contains 2 million drawings and sketches and 600,000 photographs, all available for visitors to peruse. Close by is **Café Blom**, see ③, a good place for a spot of refreshment.

Östasiatiska Museet

The third museum reached by crossing Skeppsholmsbron is located at the island's northern tip on Tyghusplan. **Östasiatiska Museet ❼** (Museum of Far Eastern Antiquities; www.ostasiatiska.se; Tue 11am–8pm, Wed–Sun 11am–5pm; free) is housed in a building dating from 1700, which was originally designed as a stable and quarters for Charles XII's bodyguards. The museum's enormous collection embraces art from Japan, Korea, India and China and includes 1,800 objects given to the museum in 1974 by the late King Gustaf VI Adolf, a distinguished archaeologist and a respected authority on Chinese art.

Highlights here include ancient Stone Age pottery, a reconstructed Chinese grave, colourful ceramics dating from the Ming Dynasty (1368–1644), and a series of highly impressive 3,000-year-old bronze sacrificial vessels. There is also a Japanese-inspired café on site.

Food and Drink

① CAFÉ SÖDERBERG

Kungsträdgården 2; tel: 08-21 71 75; www.cafesoderberg.se; summer: daily 8am–11pm, winter: 10am–7pm; $
Lovely spot to watch the world go by while tucking into a hot cheese and ham sandwich or a Malaysian chicken curry. In summer perhaps choose a prawn sandwich instead, Swedish style.

② RESTAURANGEN MODERNA MUSEET

Moderna Museet; tel: 08-520 236 60; www.modernamuseet.se; open as museum hours; $$
Whether you want a sturdy lunch, a refreshing juice or a croissant with your coffee you will not be disappointed at this restaurant boasting stunning city views. Brunch is served at weekends and there is a children's menu too.

③ CAFÉ BLOM

Exerciseplan 4; tel: 08-527 546 50; www.cafeblom.se; Tue, Fri 11am–7.30pm, Wed–Thu 11am–5.30pm, Sat–Sun 11am–5.30pm; $
Located by the Picasso Garden and close to ArkDes, this café serves light lunches, pastries, coffees and craft beers from local breweries. The bread is organic and locally produced and vegetarians are well catered for. There's outdoor seating in the summer.

Step back in time at Skansen

WEST DJURGÅRDEN

Turn the clock back to celebrate Nordic history on the lush island of Djurgården, continuing with visits to some of the most diverse and excellent museums Stockholm has to offer. There really is a museum for every taste.

DISTANCE: 3km (2 miles), plus walking around Skansen Open Air Museum
TIME: A full day
START: Nordiska Museet
END: Djursgårdsbron
POINTS TO NOTE: To get to the Nordiska Museet, just over Djursgårdsbron, take bus No. 67, 69, 76 or No. 7 tram from Sergels Torg. There are also ferries to Djurgården.

Stockholmers love Djurgården and it's easy to see why. This immense, largely unspoiled island of natural beauty used to be a royal hunting ground and is still controlled by the king to this day. Enjoy its outdoor coffee shops and restaurants, amusement park and wonderful array of museums ranging from ships to pop music. In summer you can also take a vintage tram (7N), which runs from Norrmalmstorg to the island.

DJURGÅRDEN MUSEUMS

For all its palatial proportions, the Renai-ssance-style **Nordiska Museet ❶** (Nordic Museum; www.nordiskamuseet.se/en; daily June–Sept 10am–6pm, Wed until 8pm, Oct–May 10am–5pm; free Oct–May Wed 5–8pm) is only a quarter of its intended size. The building was designed by Isak Gustav Clason and opened in 1907. The museum was created by Arthur Hazelius (1833–1901), also the founder of Skansen (see below). In 1872 he started to collect objects that would preserve the old Nordic farming culture for future generations. Today the Nordiska Museet portrays everyday life in Sweden from the 1520s to the present, with more than 1.5 million exhibits. This grand attic is full of treasures, from luxury clothing and priceless jewellery to items such as furniture and children's toys, and replicas of period homes.

As you enter stairs lead to the huge Main Hall, where you are greeted by a gigantic statue of King Gustav Vasa, carved in painted and gilded oak by Carl Milles (1875–1955) in 1924. Temporary exhibitions are located here. The next level up (Level 3) houses the fash-

Customary wooden house

Nordiska Museet

ion gallery, the Strindberg Collection, dolls' houses, table settings, jewellery and traditional items such as the bridal crown. On the fourth floor are sections on furniture, Swedish homes, and small objects, as well as a gallery relating to the Sami people and culture. The fascinating dolls' houses show typical homes from the 17th century to modern times. A traditional table setting from the 17th century is truly remarkable. The Strindberg Collection also includes 16 paintings by the author and dramatist (1849–1912), including *Snowstorm at Sea* (1894). The Lekstugan (Playhouse) on Level 2 is a fun place for children to dress up and experience life in the olden days.

Nautical wonders at Vasa Museum

Junibacken

From the museum head west through Galärparken to **Junibacken** ❷ (Galär-varvsägen; www.junibacken.se; May–Aug daily 10am–5pm, Jan–Apr, Sept–Dec Tue–Sun 10am–5pm), a cultural centre devoted to children's literature, in particular to Astrid Lindgren (see page 120). This highly popular museum also includes a mock-up of a station and mini-train ride to meet some of Lindgren's characters, especially the most loved, Pippi Longstocking.

Vasa Museum

Leaving the museum, head south along the waterfront to the **Vasamuseet** ❸ (Vasa Museum; www.vasamuseet.se; daily June–Aug 8.30am–6pm, Sept–May 10am–5pm, Wed until 8pm). The city's most popular museum, it houses the *Vasa*, the royal warship that capsized in Stockholm's harbour on 10 August 1628 in calm weather just 1,300m (4,265ft) into her maiden voyage. About 50 people died on the ship that was supposed to be the pride of the navy. Only some of the guns could be salvaged from the vessel at the time and it was not until 1956 that the persistence of marine archaeologist Anders Franzén led to the rediscovery of the *Vasa*. After the subsequent salvage operation, the museum opened in 1990 less than a nautical mile from where the *Vasa* sank.

As you walk into the dark interior of the museum, taking in its fragrant wood aroma, you will be immediately struck by the magnificence of the ship, which is amazingly well preserved. The *Vasa* has gold leaf on her poop and bow, guns of bronze, and is decorated with 700 sculptures and carvings. On that fateful August day in 1628, as the *Vasa* set sail from Stockholm, a sudden gust of wind struck; the ballast was not heavy enough to balance the weight of the heavy artillery on the upper gun deck, so water flooded through the gun ports and the ship keeled over and sank, drowning 30–50 crew members.

The salvage operation is brought to life in a film – some 24,000 objects were rescued, including skeletons, sails, cannons, clothing, tools, coins, butter, rum and numerous everyday utensils. You can see many of these objects and some, such as a sailor's *kista* (chest), containing his pipe, shoe-making kit and all the other necessities for a long voyage, are quite poignant.

Spritmuseum

From Vasamuseet, continue along Djurgårdsvägen south to find the **Spritmuseum** ❹ (Museum of Spirits; www.spritmuseum.se; Mon 10am–5pm, Tue–Sat 10am–7pm, Sun noon–5pm), a unique museum all about the Swedes' bittersweet relationship with alcohol. A visit to the museum bar is, of course, a must. Spritmuseums Restaurang (see page 103) here is noted for its creative Nordic cuisine. Continuing south, the small **Aquaria vattenmusem** on the right will please visitors interested in ocean creatures.

Ultimate ABBA experience   *Spinning around at Tivoli Grona Lund*

Liljevalchs Konstall

Heading along Djurgårdsvägen you will find on your right the newly renovated **Liljevalchs Konsthall** ❺ (www.liljevalchs. se; Tue–Sun 11am–5pm, until 8pm Tue and Thu), one of Northern Europe's most attractive art galleries, which was built in 1913–16 in the then popular neoclassical style. Next door is **Blå Porten**, see ①, a lovely place for an alfresco lunch.

ABBA: the Museum

A little further down Djurgårdsvägen the museum devoted to the Swedish pop group ABBA has been a hit since it opened in 2013. **ABBA: the Museum** ❻ (www. abbathemuseum.com; daily 10am–6pm, with exceptions; tickets can be booked online to avoid queues) is a modern interactive museum, showcasing the ever-popular group's work. You can even experience what it would be like to be the group's fifth member by auditioning in a replica of the band's Polar Studios and record your own music video. It's a dream place not only for ABBA fans but for all music lovers who can learn so much more about Swedish pop. Inside the museum, **Pop House**, see ②, makes for a good lunch or coffee stop.

AMUSEMENT PARK

Continue along Djurgårdsvägen to **Gröna Lund Tivoli** ❼ (tel: 010-708 91 00; www.gronalund.com; May–Sept and over Christmas, hours vary so check ahead), an attractive amusement park with roots in the 18th century. If you are

travelling with children, or have a weakness for thrills, try to fit this into your itinerary. In addition to its spectacular setting, rides, roller coasters, shooting galleries and numerous restaurants, fast-food outlets and bars, it has a first-rate theatre and open-air stage where top Swedish and international entertainers perform.

SKANSEN

Cross Djurgårdsvägen to the main entrance of **Skansen** ❽ (tel: 08-442 80 00; www.skansen.se; hours vary throughout the year, check website). This is the world's first open-air museum, opened in 1891 by Arthur Hazelius, who wished to preserve the pre-industrial Swedish way of life. Hazelius collected traditional buildings from across Sweden – Skansen features some 150 of them, including an 18th-century church, **Seglora Kyrka**, which is still used for services and is a popular venue for weddings.

Take the escalator up to the Town Quarter, where original wooden town houses have been grouped together to replicate a medium-sized 19th-century town. Glass blowers, shoemakers and other craftsmen demonstrate their skills in restored workshops. The smell of *kanelbullar* (cinnamon buns) may lure you into the bakery.

Leaving the Town Quarter, walk to **Skogaholm Herrgård**, a 17th-century estate relocated from an ironworks village in central Sweden. Stroll to Tings-vallen/Bollnästorget, the venue for the

An old-fashioned farmstead at Skansen

Christmas market and midsummer celebrations, where you can buy the traditional Skansen treat of waffles topped with berry jam and cream. Head west to peer into the Älvros Farmhouse. In the northern part of the park, Vastveit Loft, a storehouse from eastern Norway, built in the 14th century, is Skansen's oldest building. Wwalk east for the zoo where you will see brown bears, wolves and elks. There is also an aquarium.

As you wind your way back to the main entrance, be sure to see **Hornborgastugan**, a timber cottage from western Sweden with a straw and peat roof. This demonstrates the living conditions of poorer people in the 19th century.

DJURGÅRDSBRON

Leave Skansen by the main Djurgårdsvägen exit, turn right and head back to **Djurgårdsbron** ❾. The bridge, opened in 1897 for the Stockholm Exhibition, is richly ornamented with cast-iron railings in the form of stylised water plants. Wrought-iron lamps and sculptures of mythical gods sit atop four granite pillars at either end, and there's a grand view of the elegant Strandvägen. Canoes, kayaks, pedaloes and bicycles can be hired from **Sjöcaféet** (Galärvarvsvågen 2; www.sjocafeet.se) not far from the bridge, which also has a **restaurant**, see ❸, bar and visitor centre.

Food and Drink

❶ BLÅ PORTEN

Djurgårdsvägen 64; tel: 08-663 87 59; www.blaporten.com; Mon–Tue, Sun 11am–7pm, Sat 11am–8pm; $$
This is a classic destination for Stockholmers on a weekend walk or on a visit to Djurgården's museums. Set in a picturesque patio garden, Blå Porten serves modern Mediterranean and local cuisine, as well as sandwiches and light options.

❷ POP HOUSE

Djurgårdsvägen 68; tel: 08-502 541 40; www.pophouse.se; Mon–Fri 11.30am–3pm, Sat–Sun 7.30–10.30am, noon–4pm; dinner daily from 5pm; $$
Part of the Pop House Hotel, this sleek restaurant in the ABBA museum combines romantic candlelit tables and twinkling lights with an industrial-style ceiling. The menu offers lunch specials and sandwiches while the dinner menu is à la carte. The airy café ($) here has quirky furniture (same hours as museum).

❸ SJÖCAFÉET

Galärvarvsvagen 2; tel: 08-661 44 88; www.sjocafeet.se; daily 9am–9pm; $$
Even if you don't want to hire a boat or a bicycle you can come here at the end of the walk for some refreshment. Relax outside in summer with a cool drink or have a hot chocolate by the fire in winter. Cakes, pastries and sandwiches or try the weekly-changing lunch menu.

A typical room at Prins Eugen's Waldemarsudde

EAST DJURGÅRDEN

The southeast of Djurgården is the location of the waterfront home and gallery of Prins Eugen's Waldemarsudde. The route takes in the Rosendal Slott and Trägårdar (gardens) before moving to Djurgården's eastern tip to view another private art collection.

DISTANCE: 3km (2 miles) for full walk; 1.5km (1 mile) plus bus to gallery
TIME: Half a day
START: Waldemarsudde
END: Thielska Galleriet
POINTS TO NOTE: To reach Waldemarsudde in summer, hop on one of the vintage trams (No. 7N) that leave from Norrmalstorg. Otherwise, bus No. 47 or tram 7 will get you there all year. This route can be combined with Route 4. Note Rosendals Slott is only open June–Aug.

The eastern side of Djurgården is less visited than the west and you can take the tram from Skansen (see page 49) on to Waldemarsudde if you have the time. However a trip to this side of the island on its own provides some interesting galleries and architecture, plus beautiful gardens and natural surroundings.

WALDEMARSUDDE

Prins Eugen's Waldemarsudde ❶ (www.waldemarsudde.se; Tue–Sun 11am–5pm, Thu until 8pm) is often called the most beautiful gallery in the city, and with good reason. Overlooking Saltsjön, Waldemarsudde was the home of Prins Eugen, the 'painter prince' and brother of the late King Gustav V. Prins Eugen, who died in 1947, bequeathed to the nation his lovely home and garden as well as his collection, which includes a number of impressive landscapes that he painted himself. Across from windows offering magnificent views of Riddarfjärden, you will find the prince's alfresco painting representing the 'Shores of Stockholm'.

The collection

Waldemarsudde has an ambitious collection of Swedish paintings, mostly from the late 19th and early 20th centuries along with sculptures by artists of the same era such as Per Hasselberg, Carl Milles, Auguste Rodin and Christian Eriksson to be found in both the gallery and the park.

Waldemarsudde is renowned for its beautiful indoor flower displays and it is a delightful house to explore. The drawing room and guest apartments remain

Picturesque Waldemarsudde

largely unchanged. The two upper floors, with the prince's studio at the top, are used for temporary exhibitions. Make sure to walk around the beautiful grounds and perhaps stop for refreshments at the **Prinsens kök** (Prince's Kitchen) see ❶, inside the house.

ROSENDALS

From Waldemarsudde, head north to Prins Eugens Väg and cross the road, continuing a short distance until you come to Djurgårdsvägen, at which you turn right and then left, heading north on Valmundsvägen. This leads to Rosendalsvägen and **Rosendals Slott** ❷ (Rosendals Palace; www. kungahuset.se; June–Aug Tue–Sun guided tours only, on the hour noon–3pm).

The palace is considered to be one of the best examples of the Empire or Karl Johan style of architecture, named after King Karl XIV Johan (1818–44). Built and designed in the 1820s as a summer retreat for the king

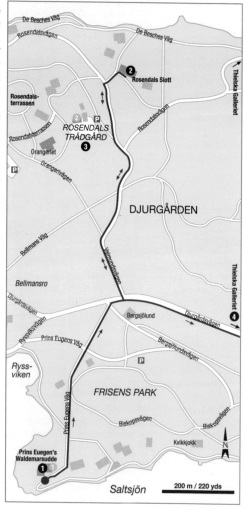

Café, Rosendals Trägård   *Orchard at Rosendals Trägård*

by Fredrik Blom, it was one of Sweden's first prefabricated homes. In 1913 it was opened to the public as a museum and it remains a highly impressive work of historic restoration. The decor is magnificent, with Swedish-made furniture and richly woven textiles in brilliant colours.

Rosendals Trägårdar

Just west of the palace is **Rosendals Trägårdar** ❸ (www.rosendalstradgard. se; Apr–Sept daily 11am–5pm; Feb– Mar, Oct– 22 Dec Tue–Sun 11am– 4pm; free), a bio-dynamic market garden run by a foundation using bio-dynamic cultivation methods and also running courses, lectures and exhibitions. There are plants for sale and you can select your own bouquet of flowers from the garden in summer.

The **café**, see ❷, serves excellent home-made food. If the weather allows, you can take your meal and sit in the apple grove. Be warned that this is a popular place for Swedes so the queues may be long at the garden café.

THEILSKA GALLERIET

Stroll east for about 500m (yards) along Rosendalsvägen to Djurgårdsbrunns-bron (bridge) to get bus No. 69 to **Thielska Galleriet** ❹ on Sjötullsbacken 6 (Thiel Gallery; www.thielska-galleriet.se; Tue–Sun noon–5pm, Thu until 8pm). If you would rather go by foot, head south back on Valmundsvagen and then east on Djurgårdsvägen (about 20 minutes).

The banker Ernest Thiel commissioned architect Ferdinand Boberg (who also designed Waldemarsudde) to design a dignified villa on Djurgården for his large and valuable collection of contemporary paintings. However, during World War I, Thiel lost most of his fortune. In 1924, the state bought his collection, which mostly covers Nordic art from the late 19th and early 20th centuries, and opened Thielska Galleriet in his villa two years later.

Food and Drink

❶ PRINSEN KÖK

Prins Eugens Vag 6; tel: 08-545 837 00; www.waldemarsudde.se; Tue–Sun 11am–5pm, Thu until 8pm; $$
A classic, established eatery that has been serving good Swedish cooking for more than 100 years. The local stalwarts such as meatballs are all here but there are other options too. The lovely heated outdoor terrace is a bonus.

❷ ROSENDALS CAFÉ

Rosendalsterrassen 12; tel: 08-545 812 70; www.rosendalstradgard.se; same opening times as Rosendals Trägårdar; $
The greenhouse café serves first-class food using both organic and bio-dynamically grown vegetables from the gardens. All the breads come from the café's bakery, baked in its wood-fired stone oven. A lovely place for a light lunch, sandwich or coffee and cake.

Enjoy a relaxed stroll along the waterfront at Strandvägen

ÖSTERMALM

From the concealed jewel of a museum, Hallwylska Museet, and the magnificent Gold Room of the Historiska Musueet, a stroll along elegant Strandvägen leads you to the eastern end of Östermalm and another collection of fine museums.

> **DISTANCE:** 4km (2.5 miles) for full walk
> **TIME:** A half to a full day depending on museum visits
> **START:** Hallwylska Museet
> **END:** Etnografiska Museet
> **POINTS TO NOTE:** To get to the Hallwylska Museet at Hamngatan 4, take the metro to T-Östermalm or bus Nos. 2, 55, 62 or 76.

The attractive and affluent residential area of Östermalm is popular for its many antiques shops and pricey boutiques. One of the most populous districts in Stockholm, it has a distinctly upper-class feel to it, and a bit of window shopping along its broad boulevards is an enjoyable way to pass an hour or two. For those interested in museums there is no shortage and an extra 15-minute walk or bus ride will take you to the eastern end of Östermalm to explore three more.

HALLWYLSKA MUSEET

Countess Wilhelmina von Hallwyl was considered more than a little strange by her contemporaries but today we should be grateful for her penchant for collecting objects both rare and commonplace, all gathered from a lifetime's travels and reunited in the **Hallwylska Museet** ❶ (Hallwyl Museum; www.lsh.se; first-floor state rooms: June–Aug Tue–Sun 10am–7pm, Jan–June, Sept–Dec Tue–Fri noon–4pm, Sat–Sun 11am–4pm; free; guided tours in English July–Aug daily 10.30am, 12.30pm, June Sat–Sun 12.30pm, Sept–May Sat 1.30pm). The countess's former residence is now the home of nearly 70,000 objects, including her furniture and personal knick-knacks, all of which she lovingly and meticulously catalogued.

She decided at a young age to transform her home into a museum, to which end she gathered a diverse range of objects for more than 70 years, in the course of journeys through Europe, Africa and the Orient. She wanted to illustrate bygone as well as contemporary forms of living, from magnificent examples of sculpture and art to the homely toothbrush and mous-

Aristocratic paintings at the Hallwylska Museet

tache twirler displayed on the bedroom dresser. Although the collection varies in quality, it never fails to fascinate.

Hallwyl home

The mansion, completed in 1898, was built for Walter and Wilhelmina von Hallwyl. It was surprisingly modern, with electricity, central heating, hot and cold water, a bath and shower, and even wood-panelled toilets. The Hallwyls donated the house to the state in 1920, and after Walter's death in 1921, Wilhelmina left complex instructions in her will as to how the museum was to be run after her death (including the exact length – to the minute – of tours). She died in 1930 and the mansion remains as it was left.

The collection

The paintings in the gallery, mostly 16th- and 17th-century Flemish, were purchased over a period of just two years which, given their sheer number, is quite astonishing. Adjoining the gallery is the family bowling alley, now a showcase for top-class glazed earthenware. A rich variety of household objects are also on display in every room, all illustrating the eccentric brilliance of the collector. In contrast with the amount of energy she expended on her passion for preserva-

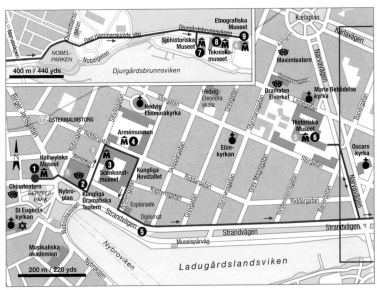

Opulence at Hallwylska Museet

tion, the countess paid scant attention to her own appearance. In a controversial portrait, displayed in the smoking room, she is dressed plainly, with virtually no jewellery, and a small moustache is clearly visible. Although her insistence on electric lighting and hot water for her bathroom was quite modern for its time, she would bathe more simply – in an old wooden tub with a bucket of water.

1896 Steinway piano

As you walk through the rooms you will notice each are decorated in the style of a different historical period – as was the fashion at the time. The main salon, in late baroque style, is built around four grandiose Gobelins tapestries and is finished in 24-carat gold leaf. The most remarkable object here is a Steinway grand piano dating from 1896, adapted to fit into its majestic setting with a casing of hardwood and inlaid wood. In 1990 it was flown to New York in two sections, weighing a total of 900kg (1,980lb) for a renovation that lasted several months. Sometimes concerts are performed on this magnificent piano, the focal point of the lavish dinners and dances that the countess was reluctantly obliged to hold a few times each year.

DRAMATEN

Leaving Hallwyska Palatset, head east on Hamngatan for about 50m (50yds) to the magnificent Jugendstil **Kungliga Dramatiska Teatern** ❷ (Royal Dramatic Theatre; see page 106), now usually referred to as Dramaten, which was designed by Fredrik Lilljekvist and opened in 1908. The façade, inspired by the Viennese architectural style, is in white marble. Christian Eriksson provided the masterful relief frieze, Carl Milles the centre section, and John Börjesson the bronze statues. These are complemented in the foyer by Börjesson's Tragedy and Theodor Lundberg's Comedy. The lavish design continues inside.

Worth seeing in particular is the ceiling in the foyer by Carl Larsson. Sweden's most famous director, the late Ingmar Bergman, regularly directed plays here before his death in 2007. You can still soak up the grand atmosphere and splendid view by stopping for coffee at **Café Pauli**, see ❶, on the Dramaten's balcony. Artist Georg Pauli (1855–1935) gave his name to the café, which displays many of his paintings.

SCENKONSTMUSEET AND ARMÉMUSEUM

Take the next left after the theatre into Sibyllegatan and on the right you will find the new **Scenkonstmuseet** ❸ (Swedish Museum of Performing Arts; www.scenkonstmuseet.se; daily 11am–6pm, Wed until 8pm) opened in early 2017. The museum is devoted to performance in dance, music and theatre with an emphasis on interactivity. The collections include some 50,000 objects ranging from costumes, musical instruments,

Scenkonstmuseet exhibit

Houses on Strandvägen

puppets, stage design models and art items. There is also a concert and performance space as well as a restaurant.

Carry on up Sibyllegatan – perhaps stopping at No 3 for a coffee or snack at **Café Tidemans**, see ② – and then turn right into Riddargatan. At No. 13 is the **Armémuseum** ❹ (Army Museum; www.armemuseum.se; June–Aug daily 10am–5pm, Sept–May Tue–Sun 11am–5pm, Tue until 8pm; free; guided tours in English June–Aug) housed in the old armoury; you can learn much about Sweden's history and its people through both peacetime and wartime over the past 500 years. Don't miss the Trophy Chamber with its unique spoils of war and trophies and get a look at a nuclear warhead.

STRANDVÄGEN

Leaving the museum turn right into Artillerigården and head down to the shore side road of **Strandvägen** ❺. The palatial houses along here were built in the early 20th century by Stockholm's 10 richest citizens, seven of whom were wholesale merchants. This was a hilly, muddy harbour area until a campaign began in advance of the 1897 Stockholm Exhibition to create a grand avenue unrivalled in Europe. This was a long process, as the old wooden quay erected in the 1860s was still a bit of an eyesore. Up until the 1940s boats would bring firewood from the archipelago islands to the quay. Eventually, Strandvägen, with its three rows of lime trees, became the elegant boulevard that had been envisioned. It is still a popular place to wander. As you walk, you'll notice some of the old wooden sailing vessels anchored along the quay, rescued by boat enthusiasts who have lovingly refurbished them. Beside every boat is a sign describing its history.

HISTORISKA MUSEET

At the corner of Strandvägen and Narvavägen, turn left, heading north on Narvavägen to the **Historiska Museet** ❻ (Swedish History Museum; www.historiska.se; June–Aug daily 10am–5pm, Sept–May Tue–Sun 11am–5pm, Wed until 8pm; guided tours in English at 1pm; free) with its spectacular Gold Room. The museum, designed by Bengt Romare and Georg Sherman, opened in 1943. Bror Marklund designed the decoration around the entrance and

Armémuseum

The Sjöhistoriska Museet offers an insight into Stockholm's naval history

the richly detailed bronze gateways. The museum has a prominent collection from the Viking era as well as from the early Middle Ages. Without doubt the most amazing sight is the Guldrummet (Gold Room), where many of Historiska Museet's gold treasures were gathered in the early 1990s for a breathtaking display. This vault, 7m (23ft) underground, was built with 250 tons of reinforced concrete to ensure security. The room is divided into two circular sections. The inner section houses the main collection, with 50kg (110lb) of gold treasures and 250kg (550lb) of silver from the Bronze Age to the Middle Ages.

These amazing exhibits come from some unexpected sources. For instance the gold collars were found between 1827 and 1864 in a stone quarry in eastern Sweden, in a ditch on the island of Öland, and on a spike in a barn. Note, too, the Elisabeth reliquary, originally a drinking goblet mounted with gold and precious stones in the 11th century. In about 1230, a silver cover was added to enclose the skull of St Elisabeth. In 1631, during the Thirty Years War, it was seized as a trophy for Sweden.

The museum makes for a fitting new premise for the collection of the Myntkabinettet (Royal Coin Cabinet Museum), formerly located on Slottsbacken opposite the Royal Palace and moving here in 2019. You will once again be able to see the displays devoted to the history of monies of the world, a thousand-year history of Swedish coinage and examples from archaeological finds throughout the centuries. A highlight is the largest coin in the world, weighing in at 19.7kg (43lbs).

If it's lunchtime then a good option is the museum's **Restaurant Rosengården**, see ③, which also serves cake and coffee if that's all you want.

EASTERN ÖSTERMALM

For those wishing to visit three national museums (maritime, science and technology and ethnography) – set in some lovely countryside by the water – walk back down Narvavägen and catch the No.69 bus at Djurgårdsbron out to the far eastern shore of Östermalm. Alternatively continue along Strandvägen for a 15-minute walk east into Djurgårdsbrunnsvägen to reach the museums.

Sjöhistoriska Museet
Set in lovely wooded countryside by the water, the **Sjöhistoriska Museet** ❼ (National Maritime Museum; www.sjohistoriska.se; Tue–Sun 10am–5pm; free) is located in a fine building designed by Ragnar Östberg, architect of the Stadshuset. The museum traces the history of the Swedish Navy and the merchant marines. The centrepiece of the collection is the stern of the schooner Amphion, which was instrumental in the victory of a key battle against the Russian Navy in 1790 under the command of Gustav III.

Kids can get interactive at the displays of Tekniskamuseet

Tekniskamuseet

Just to the east of the maritime museum is **Tekniskamuseet** ❽ (National Museum of Science and Technology; www.tekniskamuseet.se; daily 10am–5pm, Wed until 8pm), a huge space with lots of 'hands-on' and interactive exhibits and experiments, including the exhibition 100 Innovations. Check out the Royal Model Chamber, displaying the inventions of Christopher Polhem (1661–1751), a genius often described as the 'Father of Swedish Technology'.

Etnografiska Museet

East of the maritime museum is the **Etnografiska Museet** ❾ (National Museum of Ethnography; www.varldskultur museena.se; Tue–Sun 10am–5pm, Wed until 8pm; free), which houses some 220,000 items brought back by Swedish travellers and scientists from the 18th century to the present day. Experience the art, culture and food from across the globe, and maybe check out the restaurant **Matmekka**, see ❹, for its fusion food.

Food and Drink

❶ CAFÉ PAULI
Nybrogatan 2 12; tel: 08-665 62 66; www.dramatenrestaurangerna.se; Mon–Fri 11.30am–2.30pm; $
Café Pauli is located on the balcony at Dramaten and has a lovely terrace overlooking Nybrogatan where the changing of the guard takes place in summer. The café serves a lunch buffet for a very reasonable price. There are other eating options in the building too.

❷ CAFÉ TIDEMANS
Sibyllegatan 3; tel: 08-664 11 70; www.tidemans.se; Mon–Fri 9am–8pm, Sat–Sun 10am–8pm; $
Situated off the beaten track behind Dramaten, come here for pizza, salads, sandwiches and more substantial mains at good prices. It's an ideal choice for breakfast too before you start your sightseeing.

❸ RESTAURANT ROSENGÅRDEN
Narvavägen 13–17; tel: 08-519 556 00; www.historiska.se; Mon–Fri 9am–8pm, Sat–Sun 10am–8pm; $
Find this restaurant in the Swedish History Museum, where you can enjoy brunch, lunch or afternoon tea. Using local, seasonal produce, there are three daily specials to choose from. Or have a coffee and a cinnamon bun overlooking the rose garden and fountain.

❹ RESTAURANT MATMEKKA
Djurgårdsbrunnsvägen 34; tel: 070-777 12 50; www.varldskulturmuseerna.se; Mon 11am–2pm, Tue–Sun 11am–5pm, Wed until 8pm; $$
Enhancing the philosophy of the Ethnography Museum it is housed in, this restaurant uses local Swedish produce in its world cuisine. It's all about the raw ingredients and what's in season.

SÖDERMALM

This neighbourhood is full of artists' studios and galleries, and also features casual chic restaurants around Nytorget. As you stroll past the old worker's cottages at Åsöberget, there are fine city and water views, and the beautiful Fjällgatan is the jewel in the crown.

DISTANCE: 3.2km (2 miles)
TIME: Half a day
START: Stadsmuseet
END: Fotografiska
POINTS TO NOTE: To start this itinerary take the metro to T-Slussen or bus Nos. 2, 3, 43, 53, 55, 59, 76 to Slussen.

The island of Södermalm, known as 'Söder' (South), is the city's largest neighbourhood, with 110,000 residents, and is the most youthful and bohemian area in central Stockholm. Söder rises sharply from the water on slopes lined with old wooden cottages, which were protected by law in the 1920s, and has some of the best views of the city. There are plenty of hilly parks and allotments in the built-up areas, and numerous shops, bars and restaurants. Indeed, the recently gentrified Söder, once the city's poorest working-class district, has more restaurants than any other part of Stockholm and the lively nightlife is a little more laid-back than in the more exclusive district of Östermalm.

STADSMUSEET

Södermalm is huge, so this itinerary is selective, but it takes in some key sights while providing a glimpse into the soul of Söder. Slussen (the Sluice Gate), is a clover-leafed roundabout above the narrow canal connecting the lake with the sea. Work commenced in 2016 on the construction of the 'New Slussen', one of the largest urban transformation projects in Sweden. Starting your walk close to the Slussen metro at **Stadsmuseet** ❶ (City Museum; closed until 2018), you are in the heart of the area being developed.

KATARINAHISSEN

Slussen is home to one of the city's most curious sights: **Katarinahissen** ❷ (Katarina Lift), which is a 38m (125ft) lift opened to the public in 1883 and still a prominent silhouette on the skyline. The original steam-operated lift switched to electricity in 1915, and in the 1930s was replaced by a new model. The lift stopped operating in 2010 due to safety

Historic townhouses, apartment buildings and boats line the waterfront of Södermalm

concerns but there are plans to renovate and reopen it in 2019. There is, however, a modern lift inside the building where the famous restaurant Gondolen (see page 105) is housed, which transports you to a public viewing gallery with amazing views over the city. Follow the temporary signs for Gondolen from outside the metro. Take the lift to the 11th floor and then carry on up one set of stairs to access the viewing gallery above the restaurant.

MOSEBACKE

From the viewing gallery, walk straight ahead to **Mosebacke Torg** ❸ with its attractive square, featuring Nils Sjögren's sculpture *The Sisters*. The Mosebacke area got its name from a miller and landowner, Moses Israelsson, the son-in-law of Johan Hansson Hök, who operated two mills on the hilltop plateau in the 17th century. Mosebacke became a centre for entertainment. A theatre built in 1852 was later destroyed by fire and then replaced in 1859 by the **Södra Teatern**, designed by Johan Frederik Åbom. Go through the gateway leading to Mosebake Terrass and enjoy another splendid view of the city.

HÄCKEJÄLL

Back in the square take the small steps on the left and head east on **Fiskargatan**, bearing right and then turning left into Svartensgatan in the Häckejäll (Hell's Forecourt) district. In the 17th century people believed that witches gathered here on the cliffs before flying to Blåkulla, where the devil held court.

Katarina kyrka

Katarina Kyrka

Refuge was often sought in the church. The buildings on Katarinaberget date partly from the 18th century, but churches have been built on this site since the early 14th century. Earlier chapels were replaced in 1656 with the more impressive **Katarina Kyrka** ❹, designed by Jean de la Vallée. King Karl X Gustav oversaw the building of the church and insisted that it should have a central nave with the pulpit in the centre. In 1723 the church was badly damaged by fire but was restored over the next two decades. A new copper roof was added in 1988. Two years later, another fire destroyed the church, sparing only the outer walls. Ove Hildemark designed a costly, mostly publicly funded restoration using 17th-century building methods. The central dome was joined with heavy timbering in the traditional way and the collapsed central arch was rebuilt with specially made bricks in 17th-century style. In 1995 the church was consecrated and many consider it more beautiful than ever.

BUTCHER'S HOUSE

Head west on Högbergsgatan and take a peek at Nytorgsgatan 5, one of the more beautiful red *söderkåkar*, then walk south on **Nytorgsgatan**. You will cross Mäster Mikaelsgata, named after Mikael Reisurer, who was the city's executioner 1635–50. When you come to Tjärhovsgatan, cross the street and check out the pink **Butcher's House** ❺

building at Nos. 36–8. It was built at the end of the 18th century and generations of butchers worked here until the municipality bought the building in the 1920s. In 1841 the building was remodelled and given its present appearance.

NYTORGET

Continue south on Nytorgsgatan, and for a break try No.38, the charmingly retro **Café String**, see ❶, whose interior furnishings are for sale. Just beyond the café turn right on Bondegatan to **Södermannagatan**. This is the city's bohemian quarter, with its galleries, artists and traditional craftspeople, and sundry workshops. Head east on Skånegatan, where there are more galleries, artists' shops, second-hand and antique stores and funky boutiques, until you reach **Nytorget** ❻, a most pleasant square with outdoor cafés and a popular park.

VITA BERGEN AND ASÖBERGET

Walk south on Malmgårdsvägen, passing the 300-year-old Werner Groen Malmgård (mansion) at No.53. Turn up Lilla Mejtens Gränd to enter **Vita Bergen** ❼ (White Mountain). As you stroll north through the park to Mäster Pers Gränd and Bergsprangsgränd, you'll come across houses built in the 18th century for harbour and factory workers. In 1736 the building of new houses was prohibited due to the risk of fire, but the

Vintage markets   *Fotografiska*

slum districts were exempted, preserving their original character.

Sofia Kyrka ❽ to the left was built early in the 20th century, and the area became a leafy hillside park. Head north out of the park on Stora Mejtens Gränd to Ploggatan, crossing Skånegatan and then Bondegatan to Åsögatan and Åsöberget. Early 18th-century wooden cottages for port workers on Sågargatan and Lotsgatan are plentiful here; **Åsöberget** ❾ offers fine views of the water and city.

FJÄLLGATAN

Head west and turn north at Erstagatan, crossing the busy shopping street Folkungagatan and then past Ersta Sjukhus (Hospital) to **Fjällgatan** ❿.

Many of the houses were built along this picturesque street after a devastating fire in 1723. Mamsell Josabeth's Steps were named after the artist Josabeth Sjöbert (1812–82). Sista Styverns Trappor is an alley of steps once known as Mikaelsgränd after a 17th-century executioner. It was renamed after the inn, Sista Styvern (The Last Penny).

Fjällgatan has a summer café, Kaffestuga, offering cold drinks, coffee and ice cream but if you fancy something more substantial, head for the vegetarian **Hermans**, see ❷, with its glass-topped veranda and fantastic view over Saltsjön (Salt Lake). Continue east along Fjällgatan for 50m/yds to the bend in the road. On the right you will find the **Söderbergs**

trappor (steps) that lead steeply down to the main road by the water, where to the right is the Fotografiska museum.

FOTOGRAFISKA

Fotografiska ⓫ (Stadsgårdshamnen 22; www.fotografiska.eu/en; Sun–Wed 9am–11pm, Thu–Sat 9am–1am; card only) exhibits works of well-known Swedish and international photographers and also hosts exhibitions throughout the year. Concerts are held here and there is also an award-winning restaurant, a café and a well-stocked shop on site.

Food and Drink

❶ CAFÉ STRING

Nytorgsgatan 38 6; tel: 08-714 85 14; www.cafestring.com; Mon–Thu 9am–10pm, Fri–Sun 9am–7pm; $
A colourful, cosy café where the hip 1950s–60s furnishings are all for sale. The weekend breakfast buffet (9am–1pm) is very popular so get here early.

❷ HERMANS

Fjällgatan 23B; tel: 08-643 94 80; www.hermans.se; daily 11am–9pm; $$
This is one for the vegetarians – and those who love beautiful views. There's no menu here: Hermans serves all-you-can-eat organic veggie buffets throughout the day. In summer, there is a plentiful veggie barbecue from the garden grill.

Drottningholms Slott

DROTTNINGHOLM

For a perfect escape from the city, take in Drottningholm's superb palace, theatre, park and Chinese pavilion, located on a small island in an inlet of Lake Mälaren. The splendid baroque park is a beautiful place for a leisurely stroll.

DISTANCE: Approx 2km (1 mile), plus strolling
TIME: Half a day, including travel time
START: Drottningholm Slott
END: Kina Slott
POINTS TO NOTE: You can drive or take public transport to Drottningholm. Take T-Brommaplan and then bus Nos. 176, 177, 301, 323. From April to October you can take the ferry Strömma Kanalbolaget (www.stromma.se) from Stradshusbron (one hour).

Just 10km (6 miles) west of Stockholm, Drottningholm's buildings and grounds are Unesco-listed. Part of the 17th-century palace is still lived in by the royal family and its extensive gardens, formal in the French style with statuary, fountains and trees, are a delight to walk around.

DROTTNINGHOLMS SLOTT

This tour starts at and centres around **Drottningholms Slott** ❶ (www.kunga huset.se; daily May–Sept 10am– 4.30pm, Apr daily 11am–3.30pm, Oct Fri–Sun noon–3.30pm, Nov–Mar Sat–Sun noon–3.30pm; gardens free; check website for times of guided tours in English). Inspired by the architecture of French châteaux, the palace has often been called a mini-Versailles. Its present appearance emerged towards the end of the 17th century, when it was considered to be one of the most lavish buildings of the time. Tessin the Elder (1615–81), who found his inspiration primarily in Italian architecture, succeeded in creating a building to glorify royal power. The project was completed by Tessin the Younger while leading 17th-century architects including Carl Hårleman and Jean Eric Rehn finished the interiors.

The interiors, which span the 17th, 18th and 19th centuries, are quite magnificent. One of the most beautiful rooms, Queen Hedvig Eleonora's State Bedroom, features a richly ornamented baroque style courtesy of Tessin the Elder. Sweden's most prominent artists and craftsmen spent 15 years decorating the room, which was eventually completed in 1683.

Stately bedroom   *The grand library*

Also impressive is Queen Louisa Ulrika's Library, designed by Eric Rehn, home to a vast and splendid collection that is a testament to the queen's patronage on art and science in 18th-century Sweden.

More information can be found at the newly renovated visitor centre near the palace where you'll also find the **Drottningholms Slottscafé**, see 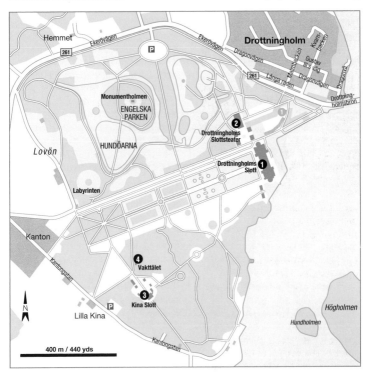, for coffee, lunch or afternoon tea.

Slottsteater

As you leave the palace, you will come to the **Drottningholms Slottsteater ❷** (Drottningholm Court Theatre; see page 106). The theatre opened in 1766 to honour Queen Louisa Ulrika, the mother of Gustav III. Gustav's two great loves were theatre and French culture and it is said that he would have much preferred to be an actor or a playwright than a king.

The Chinese Pavillion, a legacy of Sweden's fascination with the Orient

But for all his enthusiasm for culture, Gustav's benevolent despotism was not popular with his unruly nobility. His assassination in 1792 at a masked ball at Kungliga Operan (the Royal Opera) inspired Verdi's Un Ballo in Maschera. On his death, the Slottsteater fell into disuse.

It was not until the 1920s that the building was used again, after Professor Agne Beijer rediscovered it, complete and undamaged, just waiting for restoration. Today its original backdrops and stage machinery are the oldest in use anywhere in the world. To attend an opera, ballet or drama here is like stepping back in time.

Park

Behind Slottsteater, the lakefront is a popular picnic spot and it's not hard to imagine generations of royals enjoying life here. As you stroll through the baroque park behind the palace, look out on one of the parterres for a bronze statue of Hercules (1680s) by the Dutch Renaissance sculptor Adrian de Vries.

Kina Slott

Southwest of the gardens is the **Kina Slott** ❸ (Chinese Pavilion; www.kunga huset.se; daily May–Aug 11am–4.30pm, Sept noon–3.30pm; guided tours June–Aug daily noon, 2pm and 4pm, Sept daily noon and 2pm, May Sat–Sun noon, 2pm and 4pm). The pavilion, a 33rd birthday present to Queen Louisa Ulrika from her husband, King Adolf Fredrik, was made in Stockholm, shipped to Drottningholm, and assembled just a few hundred metres behind the palace. After about a decade, it was taken down and replaced. The polished tile building was designed by Carl Fredrik Adelcrantz, of Slottsteater fame.

The Kina Slott is a legacy of the era's fascination with China, after the newly formed East India Company made its first journey there in 1733. After a complete renovation in the early 1990s, it can now be seen in its original state.

More buildings

Alongside the Kina Slott is the **Confidence Pavilion**, where the king could take his meals undisturbed. The food was firstly prepared in the basement, the floor opened up and the dining table pulled up for the king and his entourage. Close by is the **Vakttälet** ❹ (Guard's Tent), which does at first glance look like a tent, but a close-up look tells a different story. In fact, it was built in 1781 to serve as quarters for the dragoons of Gustav III, and the intent was to make it look like a 'tent in a Turkish army camp'.

The Roman-style Copper Tent in winter

HAGAPARKEN

Located just to the north of the city centre, Hagaparken is part of Ekoparken, the world's first national park. This is a perfect place to wander and take in the royal palace and the exotic butterfly house and aquarium.

DISTANCE: 3km (2 miles)
TIME: Half a day
START: Haga Norra (northern gate)
END: Kinesiska Pagoden
POINTS TO NOTE: Take metro to T-Odenplan then bus 515 to the park gate; it is possible to walk to Hagaparken from the city centre, 4km (2.5 miles), or in high summer take the hop-on-hop off Brunnsviken boat from Haga Södra.

In the mid-18th century King Gustav III commissioned the architect Frederik Magnus Piper to create a royal English-style park with some unusual buildings in the popular Haga area of the city. Today Hagaparken is at the centre of Ekoparken (see page 11) and provides an escape for communing with nature, taking a picnic and immersing yourself in the cultural heritage of the city.

HAGAPARKEN

Leave the bus at Haga Norra, the northern gate, to enter Hagaparken (open all year dawn to dusk; free).

The park is best enjoyed via a stroll down its serpentine paths, which lead you to one architectural surprise after another.

Haga Parkmuseum

Among these striking buildings are the **Koppartälten** bright blue and gold Roman-style battle tents, designed by Louis-Jean Desprez and completed in 1790, and once used as stables and accommodation. The middle tent now houses the **Haga Parkmuseum ❶** (www.sfv.se; mid-May–Sept daily 11am–5pm, Oct–mid-May Fri–Sun 10am–3pm; free), which has interesting exhibitions about the park and its buildings. The east tent houses the **Koppartälten Café**, see ❶; the third tent is used for conferences and private parties.

Fjärilshuset & Haga Ocean

The park's newest attraction, located to the rear of the tents, is the **Fjärilshuset & Haga Ocean ❷** (Butterfly House and Aquarium; www.fjarilshuset.se; Mon–Fri 10am–4pm, Sat–Sun 10am–4pm),

Hagaparken at dawn

where hundreds of exotic butterflies fly freely around greenhouses in a humid tropical rainforest environment. Also here is the huge aquarium with sharks and reef fish, and the permanent exhibition 'Dangerous Animals'.

Haga Slott

Continuing east is **Haga Slott** ❸ (not open to the public), which was built in 1802–4 for Gustav IV Adolf and was the childhood home of the present king, Carl XVI Gustav and his sisters. The palace underwent extensive renovation for the Crown Princess Victoria and her new husband who made their home here in 2010.

A royal palace inspired by Versailles in France was also planned but construction was halted after the king's death. You can see the foundation of the building to the west of Haga Slott, which is fascinating in itself. **Ekotemplet** ❹, to the southeast, also designed by Louis-Jean Desprez in the 1790s, served as a royal dining room in the summer.

Gustav III's Pavilion

The lawn stretching down from Koppartälten to Brunnsviken water is called Stora Pelousen, and is a popular spot for sunbathing and picnics in the summer, and for skiing and sledging in winter. Just at the rear of the lawn and south of the palace is **Gustav III's Paviljong** ❺ (www.kungahuset.se; June–Aug Tue–Sun, guided tours in English 3pm), a Gustavian masterpiece designed by Olof Tempelman, with Louis Masreliez as the interior designer.

The 18th century's fascination with anything Chinese led to the construction of the **Kinesiska Pagoden** ❻ (Chi-

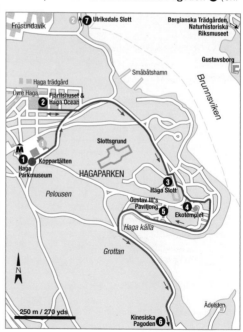

The Echo Temple   *Winter in the park*

nese Pagoda), which you will find about 700m/yds further south in the park.

FURTHER NORTH

Just north of Hagaparken is Ekoparken's most northerly treasure, **Ulriksdals Slott** ❼ (Ulriksdal Palace; www.kungahuset.se; July–Aug daily noon–4pm, May–June, Sept–Oct Sat–Sun noon–4pm, guided tours in English 3pm). By car from Hagaparken to Ulriksdals takes around 10 minutes or take bus 607 from the Haga Norra gate to Järva Krog and then it's a 20-minute walk to the palace. Alternatively from central Stockholm take metro red line T14 from the city towards Mörby, alighting at Bergshamra, then bus 503 to the palace entrance, where you will find one of the city's best-known restaurants, **Ulriksdals Wärdshus**, see ❷.

Across the water

Large parts of Ekoparken are spread around the Brunnsviken inlet. Across the water from Hagaparken you will find three other major attractions: Bergianska Trädgården (Botanical Gardens; www.bergianska.se; Mon–Fri 11am–4pm, Sat–Sun 11am–5pm; gardens free, conservatory charge), established in 1790 and featuring over 9,000 types of plants in beautiful natural settings; the Naturhistoriska Riksmuseet (Swedish Museum of Natural History; www.nrm.se; Tue–Sun 10am–6pm, Thu until 8pm, Sat–Sun 11am–7pm), founded in 1730 by the botanist Carl von Linné as part of the Academy of Sciences, and one of the 10 largest museums of its kind in the world; and the Cosmonova, which features both a planetarium and an IMAX cinema. To reach these sights take the subway to Universitetet from central Stockholm and follow the signs.

Food and Drink

❶ KOPPARTÄLTEN CAFÉ
Hagaparken; tel: 08-643 94 80; daily May–Sept 10am–5pm, Oct–Apr 11am–4pm; $
Pop inside this 'Turkish' tent for a choice of homemade cakes, pastries, sandwiches and a selection of lighter meals such as red lentil soup with grilled vegetables or pasta Bolognese. Gluten-free bread and cakes are available.

❷ ULRIKSDALS WÄRDSHUS
Ulriksdals Slottspark; tel: 08-85 08 15; www.ulriksdalswardshus.se; Mon 11.30am–4pm, Tue–Fri 11.30am–10pm, Sat 11.30am–11pm, Sun 1–9pm; $$$
Come to this lovely 19th-century inn for a special treat. Delightfully set in the park by the water this classic restaurant serves a first-class *smörgåsbord*, along with some fabulous mains and superb desserts, such as rum babas with whipped cream and raspberry preserve.

Sculptures at Millesgården museum

MILLESGÅRDEN

Carl Milles, one of Sweden's foremost sculptors, chose the lovely island of Lidingö to build his residence and studio, complete with a series of stunning terraces, gardens and towering sculptures.

DISTANCE: 7km (4 miles) northeast of Stockholm
TIME: Half a day with travel
START/END: T-Ropsten metro
POINTS TO NOTE: Take the metro to T-Ropsten, then bus Nos. 201, 202, 204, 206, 211, 212 or 221 to Torsvik Torg and follow signs to Millesgården (300m/yd).

Carl Milles (1875–1955) was one of the 20th century's most eminent sculptors. From 1931 to 1951 he lived in the United States, where he became famous for monumental sculptures such as the *Meeting of the Rivers* in St Louis and the *Resurrection* fountain in the National Memorial Park outside Washington DC. Fifteen of his public works can be seen in Stockholm, including the *Orpheus* fountain in front of Konserthuset at Hörtorget (see page 40).

In 1906 he bought land on the island of Lidingö to build a house, designed by Karl Magnus Bengtson in 1908. Milles lived here with his artist wife until 1931 and again after his return from the US.

HOUSE AND GARDEN

Having left the metro **T-Ropsten ❶** and taken the bus across the bridge to Torsvik, it will take just a few minutes to locate the impressive **Millesgården ❷** (www.millesgarden.se; May–Sept daily 11am–5pm, Oct–Apr Tue–Sun 11am–5pm), a hillside 'cascade' of buildings from different eras and architectural styles. The entry portal and two of the colonnades were rescued when Gustav Adolfs Torg's Hotel Rydberg and the former opera

---

Food and Drink

❶ MILLESGÅRDEN LANTHANDEL
Herserudsvägen 28; tel: 08-446 75 93; www.millesgardenlanthandel.se; daily 11am–5pm, closed Mon in winter; $$
The café/restaurant in the middle terrace of the sculpture park has a selection of lunch dishes, coffees, teas and cakes. There are good-value, weekly specials: choose from grilled salmon or vegetarian risotto, or try the Lindingö cinnamon bun.

The terraced sculpture park at Millesgården

house were torn down. The house covers a total of 18,000 sq m (193,750 sq ft) and includes Milles' studios with originals and replicas of his work.

The lovely terraced sculpture park provides the setting for replicas of Milles' best works. On display are some of his most popular pieces – *Man and Pegasus, Europa and the Bull* and the spectacular *Hand of God*. There is also a collection of Greek and Roman sculpture.

The restaurant **Millesgården Lanthandel**, see ❶, is located on the middle terrace in the Sculpture Park where you can enjoy a snack on the outdoor terrace in summer and by the fire inside in winter.

ANNES HUS

In the late 1940s Milles's half-brother, Evert Milles, designed the low bungalow-type building on the lower terrace. This is Annes Hus the house of Milles' assistant, Anne Hedmark, whose interior design – by Josef Frank – is still intact.

Carl and his wife Olga spent their summers here after their return to Europe in 1951 and it was here in the music room that Milles died in 1955.

At Carl's bequest, Anne lived here until 1986, after which the house was used for occasional guests or official visits until it was opened to the public in 1991.

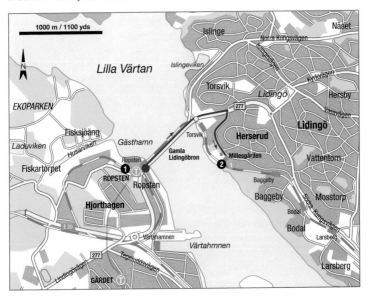

Fjäderholmarna waterfront at dusk

FJÄDERHOLMARNA

Just a 25-minute boat ride east will bring the enchanting Fjäderholmarna islands to the city's doorstep. The main island is a perfect getaway with an attractive harbour, stunning natural landscape, restaurants and handicraft shops.

DISTANCE: 1km (half a mile), plus exploring
TIME: Half a day to a full day including boat trip
START/END: Nybroplan/Slussen boat terminals
POINTS TO NOTE: Boats to Fjäderholmarna are run by Stromma from Nybroplan and Fjärderholmslinjen (www.fjaderholmslinjen.se) from Slussen – they only operate from May to early September.

The islands of Fjäderholmarna (www. fjaderholmarna.se), incorporated into Ekoparken, the National City Park in 1995, have always been a popular destination for Stockholmers as it is the closest archipelago to the centre of town. But while today's visitors head for the cliffs to sun themselves or to the restaurants to dine on fresh seafood, in the 1600s fishermen stopped here for one thing only: a glass of snaps, Swedish spiced vodka.

Explore by boat

Relax by the water and enjoy the stunning views at Fjäderholmarna

Literally, 'Fjäderholmarna' means 'The Feather Islands', but the name has nothing to do with feathers – it comes from the Swedish word *fjärdern*, which means 'bay'. Sweden's last remaining gas-powered lighthouse is on Liberty Island, but the third island, Ängsholmen, has a less illuminating claim to fame – it served as the dumping site for the city's latrines in the late 19th century. Now the island, which is owned by the king, has regained its natural beauty and the residents of its few houses live there by royal permission.

STORA FJÄDEHOLMEN

This route focuses on the quaint island of **Stora Fjäderholmen**. Although the largest of the group of four islands,

Stora Fjäderholmen only takes about 30 minutes to walk right round. It is heavily wooded in the centre but does boast a small beach. It was the last place at which fishermen could stop for a drink before they came into town with their goods. It also housed the first tavern on the journey home where snaps was sold for less than the usual price by the 'snaps king', L.O. Smith. The tavern became very popular and an outlook tower with a restaurant was added, but the tower was torn down in the 1940s and the tavern was closed during World War II when the area was taken over by the military and landing was forbidden. Access to the public was restored in the mid-1980s and some 200,000 people now visit the island every year and frequent the historic inn (see below), now famous for its seafood.

Distillery and Museum
Start your walk at the **boat terminals ❶**. Just southwest of here is a warehouse occupied by **Mackmyra ❷** (www.mackmyra.se), an outpost of Sweden's first malt whisky distillery, with guided tours and tastings in summer. Head back the way you came and soon the road passes **Restaurang Rökeriet**, see ❶, a popular fish

Island hopping in the archipelago

and seafood restaurant, and then continue southeast. Shortly, off the road to the left, is the historic tavern **Fjäderholmarnas Krog**, see ❷. Next back along the main road south is the **Allmogebåtar** ❸ museum devoted to traditional and recreational boating.

Handicraft shops

Soon you will come to a cluster of the island's quirky **handicraft shops** ❹ and workshops, ideal places to pick up a souvenir for a family member or friend. Various handicrafts are practised on the island, including metalwork, weaving, textile printing, woodcarving, pottery and glass making. There is also a small art gallery here where you are able to purchase local artwork.

Potter at work on Fjäderholmarna

Next, continue your journey southeast for breathtaking views off the coast at **Angbåtsbryggan** ❺ and then return to the craft shops and carry on southwest around the island following the coasal path. Stop for a delicious, well earned ice cream at **Röda Villan** ❻, on the northwest corner of the island. Before you board the boat back, you could take a dip in the refreshing waters of the Baltic and relax on the rocks, enjoying the last of the sun while you wait.

Food and Drink

❶ RESTAURANG RÖKERIET

Fjäderholmen 12; tel: 08-716 50 88; www.rokerietfjaderholmarna.se; May– early Sept daily noon–11pm; $$$
With a lovely view over the harbour, Rökeriet is popular with locals as well as visitors. It's a good quality, if pricey, restaurant specialising in fish and seafood with *skagen* (Swedish prawn salad) a great choice; but meat eaters are well catered for, too.

❷ FJÄDERHOLMARNAS KROG

Stora Fjäderholmen; tel: 08-718 33 55; www.fjaderholmarnaskrog.com; May–Sept daily noon–11pm (mid–late Sept Wed– Sun only); $$$
There are fabulous views from this sophisticated restaurant. It's certainly not a cheap option but the seafood is second to none; try the seafood stew.

The bustling waterside town of Vaxholm

VAXHOLM

The archipelago's main centre Vaxholm (25km/16 miles northeast of Stockholm) has been a strategic point for ships since the 19th century. The charming waterfront town is well worth exploring, and the hour long boat trip to get there is delightful.

DISTANCE: 1km (half a mile), plus further exploring
TIME: Full day including travel
START/END: Vaxholm boat terminal
POINTS TO NOTE: You can drive to Vaxholm or take the Waxholmsbolaget (www.waxholmsbolaget.se) boat from Strömkajen or the Stromma boat from Strandvägen (Apr–Dec)

The urban area of Vaxholm is the traditional trading centre for the 60 or so islands in the eastern archipelago. Vaxholm retains numerous charming reminders of life in the mid-18th century, when the wealthier Stockholmers began to turn it into an ideal resort and build elegantly decorated wooden summer homes.

As well as sightseeing and shopping you can also sail, canoe, windsurf or swim at several good bathing beaches (Eriksö and Tenö). Fishing for your own Baltic herring from the town's quayside is popular, but you could just sample them for lunch in one of the restaurants in the harbour.

FÄSTINGS MUSEET

In 1548 Gustav Vasa ordered the nearby island of Vaxholmen to be fortified, which is easily reached by small ferry (and where the route begins) close to where the boats dock. About 300 years later a new fortress was built there, but it lost its military importance and became a civil prison. Today the Kastellet citadel features the **Fästnings Museet ❶** (Vaxholm Fortress Museum; www.vaxholmsfast ning.se; June daily noon–4pm, July–Aug 11am–5pm, Sept Sat–Sun noon–5pm, May Sat–Sun noon–4pm), revealing the citadel and its defences during wartime. You can also visit the prison and an exhibition on weapons and uniforms.

VAXHOLM CENTRE

Back on Vaxholm, the wooden buildings with boutiques and craft shops around the main square and along Hamngatan make for a pleasant stroll. Start on Strandgatan, heading north away from the harbour, passing the **Waxholms Hotell ❷**. With its beautiful view of the

busy harbour, the hotel is a great place to dine – herring is a speciality – or have coffee. There are a number of other recommended spots for lunch, including **Bistro Magasinet**, see 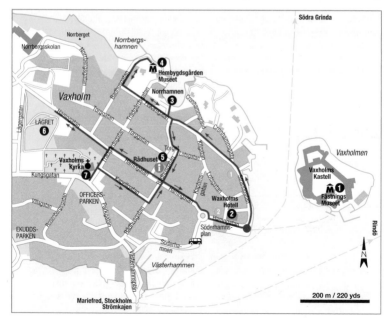 ❶, on Fiskaregatan, which has a terrace that looks over the fortress. Magasinet is both a restaurant and lifestyle store with Scandinavian furnishings and clothing, and includes a yoga studio.

Other highlights
Heading northwest on Fiskaregatan you will come to **Norrhamnen** ❸, Vaxholm's original fishing harbour featuring houses and cottages from the 19th century. It is well worth stopping at the **Hembygdsgården Museet** ❹ (Homestead Museum), set in a century-old fishing cottage with a pleasant café (museum: June–Aug Fri–Sun, also Thu and Mon in July; free; café: May–mid-Sept 11am–8pm). Here you can find out how a fishing family lived in the 1850s when around 50 families were involved in the herring industry. Back on Fiskaregatan, turn right down Norrhamsgaten, keeping to the left into Rådhusgatan, to visit the **Rådhuset** ❺

Vaxholm's waterfront in winter

(Town Hall and tourist office; www.vax holm.se/turistwebb; June–Aug Mon–Fri 10am–6pm, Sat–Sun 10am–4pm, May, Sept daily 10am–3pm, Oct–Apr Mon–Fri 10am–3pm, Sat–Sun 11am–3pm; guided tours of Vaxholm available and bicycle hire), the 100-year-old law-courts' building, given its present appearance by Cyrillus Johansson in 1925.

Continue on **Rådhusgatan** where there are several fine boutiques selling textiles, clothing, ceramics, crafts and souvenirs. Turn west on Hamngatan to **Lägret ❻**, which in 1878 was the exercise area for the soldiers manning the fortress. The large cottage on the hill was built as a residence for soldiers in 1909.

Exploring Vaxholm

Vaxholms Kyrka

Just before Lägret turn down Kungsgatan and at No.6 you will find **Vaxholms Kyrka ❼**. The present church, built between 1760 and 1803, replaced a wooden affair built in the 17th century. It's a typical Swedish church with an unusual red bell tower. Cross over to Kapellgatan, turn left and then right into Hamngatan. No trip to Vaxholm is complete without afternoon tea at the charming **Café Silltruten**, see ❷, at No. 4. Continue south back to the ferry point.

Food and Drink

❶ BISTRO MAGASINET

Fiskaregatan 1; tel: 08-541 305 05; www.magasinetvaxholm.se; daily 11am–4pm; $

Located on the third floor of this old forge devoted to lifestyle, the bistro offers a weekly lunch menu at a very good price as well as plenty of cakes and good coffee. The outdoor seating offers fine views of the island.

❷ CAFÉ SILLTRUTEN

Hamngatan 4; tel: 08-541 300 73; daily 11am–4pm; $

A proper Swedish café with odd crockery and traditional decor, this is the perfect place for exceptional coffee and yummy cakes when visiting Vaxholm. Lunch options come in large portions – great value for money.

Sunny Birka

BIRKA

Birka is a journey back in time to the days of the Vikings. Extensive archaeological discoveries on this island in Lake Mälaren reveal a great deal about life in the 8th century.

DISTANCE: 30km (19 miles) west of Stockholm
TIME: A full day
START/END: Stadshusbron boat terminal
POINTS TO NOTE: Birka is only open May–Sept; the boat trip is run by Stromma and takes two hours, best to pre-book online.

It's a picturesque boat trip to Björkö (Birch Island), one of Lake Mälaren's 300 islands. This was the site of Birka – Sweden's first Viking town and earli-est trading centre. A millennium after the Viking era, Birka has risen again, this time as part of Sweden's cultural landscape and a Unesco World Heritage site.

BIRKA

Founded in the mid-8th century, **Birka ❶** (www.birkavikingastaden.se) flourished as Europe's northernmost mercantile centre for nearly 200 years. In its heyday it had about 700 inhabitants. No one knows why Birka was abandoned but the growth of trading towns such as Sigtuna is thought to be behind its demise. The

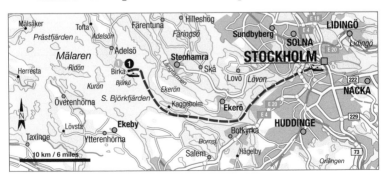

Birka museum model   *Guide at Birka*

discoveries at Birka are evidence of the elaborate trading networks of the Viking age. They portray a society of traders, merchants and skilled craftsmen. The coins, silks, beads, pottery, glass and jewellery found in 3,000 burial mounds around the town reveal links that reached the Byzantine Empire and China.

The town was planned with remarkable simplicity. People lived in modest longhouses that stood in rows overlooking the jetties where ships were moored. These were the vessels in which the Vikings, the warriors of King Svea, sailed on their marauding expeditions. The year 830 was a pivotal one in Scandinavian history, when a monk named Ansgar came to Birka, bringing with him the Christian faith. Until then Sweden had been one of the last outposts of paganism in Europe. Missionaries feared the Vikings, while in Birka the people attributed their success to their pagan gods and saw no reason to renounce them.

He was actually welcomed in Birka, probably because the people believed it would help to promote trade with Christian lands. But Christianity would not defeat the pagan gods for another 250 years, when the Viking age came to an end as a result of its refusal to tolerate rival divinities. On the crest of the hill fort on Birka stands the **Ansgar cross**, erected in 1834 to mark 1,000 years since the arrival of Ansgar at Birka. From here, across the skerry to the north, you can see Adelsö church and the ruins of the Viking-age royal court, Hovgården.

Museum

Archaeologists who work at Birka bring its fascinating history alive through animated and knowledgeable guided tours. Make sure to visit the excellent **Birka museum** (May–Sept; open when boat passengers are in) when you first arrive, if you have time, so that your imagination is working even before you begin the tour. The museum complements the archaeological finds in showing how Birka would have looked in its heyday. The opportunity to see artefacts from excavations and reconstructed Viking homes is part of what makes a visit to Birka unique. If you want to explore on your own be sure to follow the numbered signs, and you can get an English language guide book from the museum. There is a good café for light snacks and also the **Restaurant Särimner**, see ❶, for more substantial meals and lovely views. This attractive island is also an ideal place for a picnic and a swim.

Food and Drink

❶ RESTAURANT SÄRIMNER

Birka; www.birkavikingastaden.se; daily late June–Aug when boats are in; $

You can eat on the wooden deck or on the patio in the garden at Birka. The food is locally sourced and the beer is from the breweries on the neighbouring islands. Special 'Little Viking' menus are available for children.

The Renaissance castle, Gripsholms Slott

MARIEFRED

This idyllic town on Lake Mälaren, 65km (40 miles) west of Stockholm, has cobbled lanes lined with specialist shops and galleries and boasts the imposing Renaissance castle, Gripsholms Slott, at the water's edge.

DISTANCE: 1km (half a mile), plus further exploring
TIME: A full day or overnight stay
START: Gripshoms Slott
END: Östra Södermanlands Järnväg
POINTS TO NOTE: From mid-May to mid-September you can travel by steamship to Mariefred (www.mariefred.info) from Stadshubron (3hrs 30 mins), but you can get there all year by train, bus or car.

Most visitors come to Mariefred for the beautiful castle and its magical setting, but there is more to this lazy, summer lake town with its attractive yellow- and red-frame houses, lovely gardens lined up in tight rows beside narrow streets and a cobblestone square.

GRIPSHOLMS SLOTT

Gripsholms Slott ❶ (Gripsholm Castle; www.kungahuset.se; mid-May–Sept: daily 10am–4pm, mid-Apr–mid-May and Oct–Nov Sat–Sun noon–3pm; guided tours in English mid-May–Sept

daily at 3pm) was intended as a residence fit for the Renaissance ruler Gustav Vasa. Approaching this splendid castle from the water is the ideal way to appreciate the extent to which Vasa's architects succeeded, mirrored like a stage set in the waters of the lake.

Whether you arrive by boat or by land, you should start your expedition with a tour of Gripsholms Slott. There was a castle on this site in the 1300s, but the

Gripsholms throne room

An example of the regal paintings on display at Gripsholms Slott

present structure was built for Vasa in the 1530s and subsequently added to and modified by nearly every succeeding Swedish monarch. The most famous of the 16th-century apartments is Duke Karl's chamber, one of finest interiors of the period in Sweden. There are some 60 rooms in all.

Home to the Kings' Widows

During the 17th century, Gripsholm was used as a dower house (a widow's property for life) by Queen Maria Eleonora (widow of Gustav II Adolf) and Queen Hedvig Eleonora (widow of Karl X). Hedvig Eleonora made considerable changes and additions, among them the Queen's

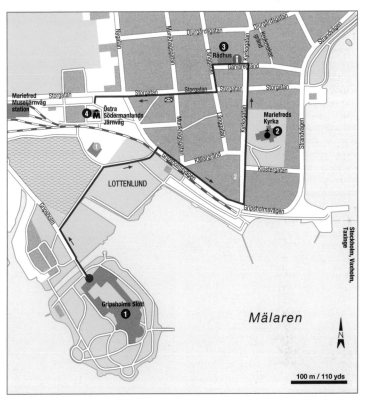

The harbour at Mariefred

Wing. The reign of Gustav III in the late 18th century marked a new period of brilliance in the castle's history. It was at this time that the exquisite theatre was fitted out in one of the round Renaissance towers. This is one of the best-preserved 18th-century theatres in Europe. Gustav III's Round Drawing Room, a counterpart to Gustav Vasa's Hall of State, dates from the same period. In the Round Drawing Room you can see portraits of Gustav III and his royal contemporaries.

In the 19th century Gripsholm evoked strong national sentiments and the castle came to be regarded as a national monument. Furniture and art of great historical importance were transferred from the various royal residences to Gripsholm to reinforce its national importance and character. A much-debated restoration of the castle took place at the end of the 19th century. Critics called it an attempt to make the castle seem to be even older than it was.

Portraits

Gripsholm is a showcase for Swedish interior design from the 16th to the late 19th century. Its unique collection of furniture and decorative arts spans 400 years. The castle is internationally known for its outstanding collection of portraits – the Swedish national collection – featuring prominent people from Gustav Vasa's day to the present. Every year, the Gripsholm Association commissions 'portraits of honour' of eminent Swedes for the collection.

Castle gardens and deer park

The grounds of the castle began life as number of small gardens that developed over the centuries. By the mid-18th century Gustav III transformed much of the land into a park. In the 19th century a more romantic style was created with trees and flowers planted and paths meandering throughout. In the 1860s Karl XV developed the land into a proper deer park, introducing fallow deer, which today number around 100. In all there is around 6,111ha (150,000 acres) for visitors to roam around and hopefully see deer up close.

MARIEFRED CENTRE

Leaving the castle, take a stroll into the quaint and delightful town, which received its charter in 1605. Walking back towards the station you might pause

Gripsholms Vardshus

Quiet Mariefred streets   *Mariefred steam railway*

for lunch at **Slottspaviljongen**, see ❶, in Lottenlund, which has a good view of Lake Mälaren. However, continuing west along Gripsholmsvägen and taking a left into Kyrkogatan, you'll find the ideal place for lunch in **Gripsholms Värdshus** (Gripsholm Inn), see ❷, built on the site of the former monastery, Pax Mariae (Maria's Peace), which gave the town its name. Gripsholms Värdshus is Sweden's oldest inn and its dining room gives a magnificent view over the castle and lake. The inn's wine cellar has remains from the 15th-century monastery. If you want to splash out, stay at the hotel (see page 97), each room of which is individually designed with period furniture and decor.

After lunch, continue walking through Mariefred, where wooden houses are situated along the cobbled lanes. Be sure to see both the early 18th-century **Mariefreds kyrka** ❷ (church) on Klostergatan and the 18th-century **Rådhus** ❸ (Law Courts) at Rådhustorget, with the tourist information office adjacent (June–Aug Mon–Fri 9am–3pm). There are also speciality shops, galleries and several good antique shops.

VINTAGE RAILWAY

Before leaving Mariefred you should take a ride on the **Östra Södermanlands Järnväg** ❹ (East Södermanland Railway; Storgatan 21; www.oslj.nu; mid-May–mid-Sept Sat–Sun, daily late June–Aug). There is a collection of rolling stock, centred on the seven Swedish railways that

ran scheduled passenger traffic on the 600mm narrow gauge track. The line was closed in 1964 but volunteers of the O.S.J. took over the line and station and re-laid the track a few years later. You can take the train from Mariefred to Läggesta, a distance of 4km (2.5 miles) at a top speed of 25km/h (12mph); it's slow but a delightful trip. You can then catch an express train back to Stockholm.

Food and Drink

❶ SLOTTSPAVILJONGEN

Gripsholm Lottenlund; tel: 0159-100 23; www.slottspaviljongen.se; June–Aug daily 11am–9pm, Apr–May & Sept Fri 5–9pm, Sat–Sun 11am–4pm; $$
This is a lovely restaurant with bright rooms and an outdoor terrace with views of the lake. It has a varied vegetarian-friendly menu with some good fish dishes, such as steamed cod, and is recommended for its excellent chips.

❷ GRIPSHOLMS VÄRDSHUS

Kyrkogatan 1; tel: 0159-347 50; www.gripsholms-vardshus.se; Mon–Sat noon–3pm, 6–9pm, afternoon tea Sat 2–4pm; $$$
With a lovely view of the castle over the water, Gripsholms has a renowned reputation but be warned the portions tend to be small albeit well prepared. Choose from fine dining or 'pub'-style dishes using with seasonal ingredients.

Walking in Uppsala

UPPSALA

History jostles you at virtually every corner in Uppsala, an ancient centre of culture, religion and education. From botanic gardens to burial mounds this city offers something a bit different.

DISTANCE: 4km (2.5 miles)
TIME: A full day or overnight stay
START: Centralstationen
END: Gamla Uppsala
POINTS TO NOTE: The city is just 40 minutes by train from central Stockholm. To reach Gama Uppsala take bus No. 2 from Uppsala centre.

This full-day excursion explores Sweden's ancient capital, Uppsala, 73km (45 miles) north of Stockholm, the last bastion of paganism and the seat of one of Europe's greatest universities. Here you'll find the country's oldest botanical garden, founded by Olof Rudbeck the Elder in 1655 and redesigned almost a century later by the renowned botanist Carl von Linné. Finally, visit the Stonehenge of Sweden at Gamla Uppsala's eerie Kungshögarna. The city is an appealing blend of ancient capital and bustling university town on the banks of the River Fyrisån, with old wooden buildings ageing gracefully and in sharp contrast to the new glass and steel structures.

UPPSALA DOMKYRKAN

Northwest from Centralstationen is the **Uppsala Tourist Office** (Kungsgatan 59; www.destinationuppsala.se; Mon–Fri 10am–5pm, Sat 10am–3pm, Sun July–Aug 11am–3pm), which will arm you with all the necessary information you will need before you set out to explore the town.

Begin your sightseeing at **Uppsala Domkyrkan ❶** (Uppsala Cathedral; www.svenskakyrkan.se; daily 8am–6pm, with exceptions; free) located at the corner of Biskopsgatan and Akademigatan. Uppsala is an episcopal see and the imposing Domkyrkan is the largest Gothic cathedral in Scandinavia. Its vaults, dating from 1435, house the shrine of St Erik, an early king who is the patron saint of Sweden, as well as the graves of other monarchs (including Gustav Vasa and his three wives), bishops, generals, and a philosopher or two. The Treasury Tower Museum (May–Sept Mon–

Uppsala Cathedral   *Graves of Gamla Uppsala*

Sat 10am–5pm, Sun 12.30pm–4pm, closes 4pm daily Oct–Apr) is located in the cathedral's northwest tower, and contains religious tapestries, silver and gold articles and other objects of historical and aesthetic interest.

UNIVERSITY MUSEUM

Cross the road to Akademigatan 3 to visit the **Gustavianum** ❷ (www.gusta vianum.uu.se; Tue–Sun 11am–4pm), an ancient, onion-domed edifice home

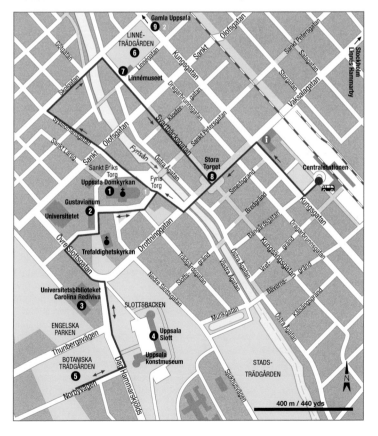

Plants at the Linnaeus Garden

to a 17th-century anatomical theatre built for the Renaissance genius Olof Rudbeck. More treasures are to be found at **Universitetsbiblioteket Carolina Rediviva** ❸ (Carolina Rediviva Library; www.ub.uu.se; closed for renovation until early 2019), which you reach after a few minutes' walk by heading southeast on Övre Slottsgatan to the intersection of Dag Hammarskjöldsväg. The building houses Sweden's oldest university library and is worth visiting for a quick peek at the 6th-century Silver Bible and other medieval manuscripts.

UPPSALA SLOTT

If you continue walking south you can't miss **Uppsala Slott** ❹ (Uppsala Castle; www.uppsalaslott.com; guided tours in English July–Aug daily 1pm and 3pm), a typically squat, imposing brick fortress from the days of the Vasa dynasty. Its main use today is as a conference centre, although a portion of it is open to the public as the **Uppsala Konstmuseum** (Uppsala Art Museum; www.konstmuseum.uppsala.se; Tue–Sun noon–4pm, Thu until 8pm; free), which exhibits contemporary art.

BOTANISKA TRÄDGÅRDEN

Across the road from Uppsala Slott is the **Botaniska Trädgården** ❺ (Botanical Garden; www.botan.uu.se; gardens: daily May–Sept 7am–9pm, Oct–Apr 7am–7pm; free; orangery: Tue–Fri 9am–3pm, also Mon July–Aug; tropical greenhouse Tue–Fri 9am–3pm, Sat–Sun noon–3pm) at Nörbyvägen 2. The garden's oldest part is baroque in style and dates back to the mid-17th century. There are more than 13,000 species and sub-species from all over the world in the garden, which has been used for teaching and research for more than 350 years.

LINNÉTRÄDGÅRDEN

After visiting the garden, retrace your steps to the cathedral. Just to the east is a good lunch stop, **Domtrappkällaren**, see ❶, at Sankt Eriksgränd 15. After lunch, continue northwest on Sysslomansgatan, turn right at Skogatan and follow the street as it crosses the River Fyris. At the intersection of Svartbäcksgatan, you will arrive at **Linnéträdgården** ❻ (www.linnaeus.uu.se; May–Sept Tue–Sun 11am–8pm, also Mon June–Aug), Sweden's oldest botanical garden established in 1655 by Olof Rudbeck the Elder. The garden has now restored the design of the botanist Carl von Linné, who became involved with it in 1745. Some 1,300 different species are arranged in beds of annuals, perennials, spring blocks and autumn blocks. Also on Svartbäcksgatan, at No. 27, is the **Linnémuseet** ❼ (Linnaeus

Linnaeus Garden   *Display at the Linnémuseet*

Museum; www.linnaeus.se; May– Sept Tue–Sun 11am–5pm, also Mon June–Aug). Von Linné and his family lived here, and today the great man's scientific activities are faithfully re-created in an 18th-century milieu, with a partially restored library, a writing room and a collection of natural history specimens.

GAMLA UPPSALA

Walk southeast on Svartbäckgatan to **Stora Torget 8**, where you can catch bus No. 2 for an excursion to **Gamla Uppsala 9**. The buses run frequently, and the trip takes about 15 minutes. Our destination is Groaplan, a 5th-century Yngling dynasty bastion. Three huge grave mounds of kings Aun, Egil and Adils (described in the opening passages of *Beowulf*) dominate the evocative cemeteries surrounding Gamla Uppsalakyrkan (Uppsala parish church). This medieval brick edifice replaced Scandinavia's last heathen temple.

Gamla Uppsala Museum
The **Gamla Uppsala Museum** (www. raa.se; May–Aug daily 10am–5pm, Sept daily 10am–4pm, Oct–Nov Mon, Wed, Sat–Sun noon–4pm) is well worth a visit. The centre focuses on the history, legends and folklore surrounding the Kungshögarna, or grave mounds, which are located just behind the museum. Armour, jewellery, weapons, textiles, everyday tools and other objects excavated from the sites are beautifully displayed in the museum. You can get an English-language map of the mounds and other ancient burial grounds from the museum. Close by is **Odinsborg** restaurant and café, see 2, where you can drink mead *(mjöd)* from old Viking ox-horns.

Summer in the outer archipelago

UTÖ

The serene beauty of the outer archipelago is dazzling, and no other island has as rich a history as Utö, which was inhabited even before the Viking era. The smaller islands surrounding it offer lovely beaches and forest paths.

DISTANCE: 50km (30 miles) southeast of Stockholm
TIME: Full day or overnight stay
START/END: Strömkajen boat terminal
POINTS TO NOTE: Only accessible by boat, take the Waxholmsbolaget boat from Strömkajen June–Aug (3h).

Renowned for its many hours of sunshine Utö is a great choice for a summer day trip or overnight. Utö is one of the finest seaside resorts in the Stockholm area with

Food and Drink

1 UTÖ VÄRDSHUS
Gruvbryggan; tel: 08-504 203 00; www.utovardshus.se; Mon–Sat noon–9pm, Sun noon–4pm; $$$
Housed in the old mining offices, this popular inn serves daily lunches as well as an à la carte menu in the evening. Fish and seafood are a highlight and there is a cheaper bar menu.

a hotel/inn, a youth hostel (Utö Vandrahem; www.utovardshus.se) and cabin, camping and B&B accommodation. You can hire bicycles, rowing boats, canoes and kayaks, and regular fishing trips and archipelago safaris are available.

MINING ON UTÖ

Utö ❶ (Outer Island; www.uto.se/en) rose out of the sea as a number of small islands at the end of the Ice Age, about 10,000 years ago. The earliest inhabitants were probably nomadic fishers and hunters with a permanent settlement here between 550 and 1050AD, by which time the whole island was inhabited and iron was being mined, an activity that went on until 1879. The Utö mines are probably the oldest, and were certainly among the most important in Sweden, with a heyday lasting over 700 years. Some of the impressive mine shafts remain; the Nyköping Mine, at 215m (705ft), is the biggest of them all.

The miners' story is told in the **Gruvmuseum ❷** (Mining Museum) next to the Utö Värdshus inn (Utö Inn; www.

Many Swedes enjoy outdoor pursuits during the warmer months

utovardshus.se). The **restaurant**, see ❶, in the inn is popular for lunch and has stunning views. Nearby, the quaint red wooden cottages along Lurgatan (now holiday homes) were the crowded, barely habitable quarters of the miners in the 18th century. It's worth climbing to the windmill (1791) for a fantastic view.

UTÖ TODAY

Today, about 200 people live on Utö year-round, but the island's population jumps significantly in the summer. The miles of bicycle paths offer an opportunity to explore. Barnensbad beach, about a 1km (0.5-mile) walk north from the **harbour** ❸ is perfect for families. The island also offers tennis courts, mini-golf and beach volleyball. Ensure you try *Utölimpa*, a thick, seeded loaf with a slightly sweet taste, which is unique to Utö.

SMALLER ISLANDS

Ålö ❹ is separated from Utö by just a bridge and you can explore it by renting a bicycle. **Rånö** ❺ and **Nåttarö** ❻ can be reached by Waxholmsbolaget ferries than run between the islands and also from the mainland at Nynäshamn. All have wonderful beaches for swimming.

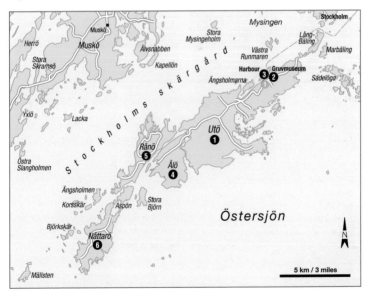

DIRECTORY

Hand-picked hotels and restaurants to suit all budgets and tastes, organised by area, plus select nightlife listings, an alphabetical listing of practical information, a language guide and an overview of the best books and films to give you a flavour of the city.

Luxurious surroudings at the First Hotel Reisen

ACCOMMODATION

Stockholm has an excellent selection of accommodation in various price ranges (but mostly in the mid-range category) and a reputation for a uniformly high standard of cleanliness, facilities and service; albeit rooms can be rather small regardless of their price category. Whether you're travelling for pleasure or on business, it is a good idea to make an early reservation and not just in high season as Stockholm is a year-round conference destination.

Hotel rates are usually lower at weekends, and come down on weekdays in high summer. Alongside international chains such as Hilton and Radisson Blu are the leading Scandinavian chains Scandic Hotels and First Hotels, both which have environmentally friendly policies. Most hotel chains offer discounts, particularly in summer. The Stockholm Visitor Centre can offer advice about accommodation options and how to book. It's worth looking into the Stockholm Package (www.destination-stockholm.com), a value-for-money deal covering around 40 hotels in a range of prices. It includes accommodation and breakfast, plus the Stockholm Pass (see page 114).

There are also plenty of youth hostels in the Stockholm archipelago for those looking at cheaper options. Most have two- and four-bedded rooms or family rooms. The hostels have self-catering facilities, but meals or snacks are provided in some. For details, contact the Swedish Tourist Federation (www.stfturist.se). The bed and breakfast system is becoming more popular in Stockholm, and you can arrange bed and breakfast accommodation in Stockholm by contacting the Bed and Breakfast Center (www.stockholm-bed-and-breakfast.se).

Gamla Stan

First Hotel Reisen
Skeppsbron 12; tel: 08-22 32 60; www.firsthotels.com; $$$
This old building is in a lovely waterfront location on Skeppsbron. Some rooms have a private spa and Jacuzzi, and there is a popular restaurant and bar.

Hotel Gamla Stan
Skeppsbron 22; tel: 08-411 95 45; www.hotelgamlastan.se; $
Overlooking Lake Mälaren on the edge of the old town, this clean and tidy hotel set in a 17th-century building has 64 rooms – some with shared bathrooms. There are family rooms available and guests have use of a kitchen.

> Price for a double room for one night including breakfast in peak season:
> $$$$ = over 3000 kr
> $$$ = 2000–3000 kr
> $$ = 1200–2000 kr
> $ = below 1200 kr

Modern tastes are catered to by Lady Hamilton

Lady Hamilton Hotel

Storkyrkobrinken 5; tel: 08-506 401 00;
www.ladyhamiltonhotel.se; $$$

This romantic option was built in 1407 and converted from a private home in 1980. Take a dip in the 14th-century basement well. The rooms, named after Swedish provincial flowers, are individually decorated with folk art and antiques.

Lord Nelson Hotel

Västerlånggatan 22; tel: 08-506 401 20;
www.thecollectorshotels.se/en/lord-nelson;
$$$

The maritime theme is well and truly alive here, with exquisite nautical antiques adorning the rooms. The tall, narrow, 17th-century building even looks like a ship. It's small and cosy, and the rooms are surprisingly light and airy.

Mälardrottningen Hotel & Restaurant

Riddarholmen; tel: 08-545 187 80;
www.malardrottningen.se; $$

Unusual and stylish accommodation on this luxury yacht (which once belonged to heiress Barbara Hutton). It is moored at Riddarholmen, not far from Gamla Stan, and features 61 elegant, well-equipped rooms. The excellent restaurant is in a splendid setting for a sunset meal.

Scandic Gamla Stan

Lilla Nygatan 25; tel: 08-517 383 11;
www.scandichotels.com;
$$$

Lots of atmosphere here among the narrow streets of Gamla Stan, with the Royal Palace, Storkyrkan and the Houses of Parliament close by. The charming rooms in this 17th-century building have recently been renovated to provide high-class comfort.

Victory Hotel

Lilla Nygatan 5; tel: 08-506 400 00;
www.thecollectorshotels.se/victory-hotel;
$$$

The Victory Hotel has an Admiral Nelson theme: a letter to Lady Hamilton is indeed one of many rare treasures to be found here. The rooms, including four suites, are elegantly appointed and each has its own interesting history. Bar, sauna and an excellent restaurant.

Modern City Centre

August Strindberg Hotel

Tegnergatan 38; tel: 08-32 50 06;
www.hotellstrindberg.se; $$

Named after the national author and artist whose statue is in the nearby park, the cosy, individually designed, en suite rooms offer very comfortable accommodation. The hotel has a courtyard and a garden.

Best Western Hotel Bentleys

Drottninggattan 77; tel: 08-14 13 95;
www.bentleys.se; $$$

In a house dating from the turn of the 20th century, and located at the top and quieter end of this famous shopping street, this charming mid-size hotel has been completely renovated.

Room at the Nordic Light Hotel

Birger Jarl Hotel

Tulegatan 8; tel: 08-674 18 00;
www.birgerjarl.se; $$$

A host of Swedish designers and artists revamped this hotel following a nature-inspired look with an emphasis on birch wood. Room 247 was overlooked however, but has since been sympathetically restored in 1970s style.

Clarion Hotel Amaranten

Kungsholmsgatan 31; tel: 08-692 52 00;
www.nordicchoicehotels.com/clarion/
clarion-hotel-amaranten; $$

Located in Kungsholmen, there is easy access from the hotel to the city centre by bus or on the subway. The excellent quality of the 423 rooms is matched by several bars and restaurants. It claims to serve Sweden's best breakfast.

Clarion Sign Hotel

Östra Järnvägsgatan 35; tel: 08-676 98 00; www.nordicchoicehotels.com/clarion/clarion-hotel-sign; $$$

This huge hotel combines the best of Scandinavian architecture and design: granite and glass reflect the street life and green park area just outside, while the design icons Egg and Swan chairs in the lobby and musical lifts add another dimension altogether. The hotel is in the heart of Stockholm adjacent to the Central Station.

Elite Hotel Adlon

Vasagatan 42; tel: 08-402 65 00;
www.elite.se; $$

Originally established in 1944, this hotel close to Central Station is now owned by the Elite chain. Housed in a charming neoclassical building, the 121 comfortable rooms are contemporary in style and there is an excellent restaurant, Kott & Fiskbaren (meat and fish bar).

Elite Hotel Stockholm Plaza

Birger Jarlsgatan 29; tel: 08-566 220 00;
www.elite.se; $$

A grand 19th-century façade fronts this pleasing hotel that was built in 1884. The 151 modern rooms are styled with warm colours. Very close to the beautiful Humlegärden Park.

Hotel Bema

Upplandsgatan 13; tel: 08-23 26 75;
www.hotelbema.se; $$

Stockholm doesn't have a great deal of budget accommodation but this lovely small hotel is a good option, well located with a pretty courtyard garden. All rooms have en suite bathrooms.

Hotel Hellsten

Luntmakargatan 68; tel: 08-661 86 00;
www.hellsten.se; $$

Located in a very trendy area, this is a suitably hip hotel where each of the 78 rooms – there are six different categories – has its own style, colour, textile design and furnishings. Almost all the junior suites boast open fireplaces and bed canopies, and seven of the rooms have balconies.

Hotel Kung Carl

Birger Jarlsgatan 21; tel: 08-463 50 00;
www.kungcarl.se; $$$

A historic family-run hotel with an attentive service. The 148 rooms vary from the traditional to the trendy and are adorned with antique clocks, mirrors and art by famous Swedish artists. In a fine central location at Stureplan.

Hotel Tegnérlunden

Tegnérlunden 8; tel: 08-545 455 50;
www.hoteltegnerlunden.se; $$$

Located in a quiet square just off shopping street Drottninggatan and a few minutes' walk from Central Station, this friendly hotel boasts a rooftop breakfast room. The renovated rooms have wooden floors and are decorated in warm neutral colours.

Nordic Light Hotel

Vasaplan 7; tel: 08-505 630 00;
https://nordiclighthotel.com; $$

A showcase for ultra-modern Scandinavian design, the 175-room hotel features 'light beds' equipped with advanced colour lighting. Great location only steps from Central Station.

Sheraton Stockholm Hotel & Towers

Tegelbacken 6; tel: 08-412 34 00;
www.sheratonstockholm.com; $$$$

This large hotel has fine views over Lake Mälaren and Gamla Stan. Spacious rooms and suites are stylishly decorated and facilities include all you would expect from this high-quality chain.

Blasieholmen and Skeppsholmen

Grand Hotel Stockholm

S Blasieholmshamnen 8; tel: 08-679 35 00;
www.grandhotel.se; $$$$

This 5-star hotel has an unparalleled view of Lake Mälaren and the Royal Palace, and attracts visiting celebrities. There's a Nordic spa and fitness centre and two Michelin-star restaurants.

Hotel Skeppsholmen

Grönagången 1; tel: 08-407 23 00;
www.hotelskeppsholmen.se; $$$$

Set on a peaceful and lush island, this 1690s house is now an award-winning hotel and offers the best of contemporary Swedish cuisine and design. Ferries regularly cross the water to Gamla Stam and the city is within walking distance.

Lydmar Hotel

S Blasieholmshamnen 2; tel: 08-22 31 60;
www.lydmar.com; $$$$

This informal and relaxed hotel between the National Museum and the Grand Hotel emphasises quality in rooms decorated with antiques and modern art. The restaurant serves delicious French-Swedish cuisine.

Radisson Blu Strand Hotel

Nybrokajen 9; tel: 08-506 640 00;
www.radissonblu.com; $$$$

Classic, elegant hotel built for the 1912 Olympics, on the waterfront at Nybroviken. The superb breakfast buffet offers locally-made produce. The hotel is per-

The Diplomat Hotel offers spacious, bright rooms

fect for spontaneous trips out to the archipelago – boats leave literally from the hotel doorstep.

STF Stockholm/af Chapman
Flaggmansvägen 8, Skeppsholmen; tel: 08-463 22 66; www.stfchapman.com; $
This would be a serious candidate for the title of the world's most beautiful youth hostel. Located on a gleaming white schooner moored off Skeppsholmen, the *af Chapman* has 136 beds and also includes the 152-bed building facing the ship's gangway. Its café has become a favourite meeting place for a beer or coffee.

Östermalm

Berns Hotel
Näckströmsgatan 8; tel: 08-556 322 00; www.berns.se; $$
This boutique-style and centrally located hotel is small and friendly. There are 65 rooms and three suites and many have a balcony with a wonderful city view. Guests have free access to a separate fitness centre. The rooftop bar serves great cocktails.

Diplomat Hotel
Strandvägen 7; tel: 08-459 68 00; www.diplomathotel.com; $$$$
This small, award-winning, family-owned hotel is on one of the most elegant avenues, facing the waterfront. Built in 1911 in classic Jugendstil it has 130 superb rooms and suites, with particularly elegant bathrooms.

Ett Hem
Söldungagatan 2; tel: 08-20 05 90; www.etthem.se; $$$$
One of the most perfect little hotels imaginable, every detail is on the nose. The decor is impeccable, and it's backed up by top-notch hospitality.

Hotel Esplanade
Strandvägen 7A; tel: 08-663 07 40; www.hotelesplanade.se; $$$$
Behind an attractive Jugendstil façade, this small, charming hotel has 34 rooms all beautifully decorated with classic Swedish furnishings and have high ceilings and parquet flooring. Excellent location overlooking Nybroviken Bay.

Villa Källhagen
Djurgårdsbrunnsvägen 10; tel: 08-665 03 00; www.kallhagen.se; $$$
A 15-minute bus ride from the centre and close to Djurgården, this pleasant hotel has 20 nature-themed rooms decorated with Scandinavian design pieces. The excellent restaurant is run by an award-winning chef.

Södermalm

Hilton Stockholm Slussen
Guldgränd 8; tel: 08-517 353 00; www3.hilton.com; $$$
This impressive modern hotel has spacious, well-equipped rooms, many of which offer spectacular views over the waters of Riddarfjärden to Gamla Stan and City Hall. It also features two restaurants, bars, a gym and a fitness centre.

Boutique elegance at Ett Hem

Hotel Anno 1647

Mariagränd 3; tel: 08-442 16 80;
www.anno1647.se; $$$
Built in 1647, this hotel retains its old-world charm and is located in Slussen, close to Gamla Stan and the ferry to Djurgården. The hotel consists of two houses linked together that blend historic character and modern interiors.

Hotel & Vandrarhem Zinkensdamm

Zinkens väg 20; tel: 08-616 81 00;
www.zinkensdamm.com; $$
The hotel is a good choice for families, with quiet rooms set apart from the bustle of the busy youth hostel ($) section. The building itself is nestled in a safe, green, leafy area.

Hotel Rival

Mariatorget 3; tel: 08-545 789 00;
www.rival.se; $$$
This boutique hotel has a cheerful colour scheme with large black-and-white photos of old Sweden on the bedroom walls. Each room also has a little teddy bear hiding somewhere in it.

Mälaren-Den Röda Båten

Söder Mälarstrand, Kajplats 10; tel: 08-644 43 85; www.theredboat.com; $
A cosy riverside hotel aboard two ships, five minutes from the Old Town. In summer the floating cafeteria Ludvigshafen offers a fine view. There are four double rooms in the hotel and 90 beds in the youth hostel ($).

NoFo Hotel

Tjärovsgatan 11; tel: 08-503 112 00;
www.nofo.se; $$
This former hostel is now a three-star hotel. Underneath the eaves, NoFo Loft (www.nofoloft.se) has simpler, cheaper rooms with shared bathrooms.

Tre Små Rum

Högbergsgatan 81; tel: 08-641 23 71;
www.tresmarum.se; $
This simple but personal hotel offers a very good-value breakfast. There are seven rooms, each comfortably and casually decorated.

Further Afield

Gripsholms Värdshus

Kykogatan 1, Mariefred; tel: 0159-347 50;
www.gripsholms-vardshus.se; $$$
The rooms of this 400-year-old inn are full of antiques and some have fireplaces or Swedish stoves (see page 83).

Hotel J

Ellensviksvägen 1, Nacka Strand;
tel: 08-601 30 00; www.hotelj.com;
$$
The rooms at Hotel J feature a nautical theme and waterfront views. The city centre is a 15-minute boat ride away.

Hotel Villa Anna

Odinslund 3, Uppsala; tel: 018-580 20 00;
www.villaanna.se; $$$
This little hotel offers comfortable, spacious monochrome rooms and a friendly welcome. Reservations necessary.

Mouth–watering burger at The Flying Elk

Bistro Pastis

Baggensgatan 12; tel: 08-20 20 18; Mon–Sat 11.30–1am; $$

This little bistro has a lovely atmosphere. The French cuisine offers very good-value, which is hard to find in this touristy area. The set-lunch menu is popular, and the crème brûlée is one of the city's best.

Bröd & Salt Bageri

Järntorget 83; tel: 08-522 468 70; www.brodsalt.se; Mon–Fri 7am–7pm, Sat 8am–5pm, Sun 9am–5pm; $

This amazing bakery is the perfect place to stop for the all-important *fika*. Its cardamom rolls are the best in Stockholm. Other branches at Birkagatan 15, Rädmansgatan 43 and Sveavägen 49.

Chokladkoppen

Stortorget 18; tel: 08-20 31 70; www.chokladkoppen.se; daily 9am–11pm (shorter hours in winter); $

The gay-friendly Chokladkoppen in the heart of Gamla Stan is a great place to warm up with a hot drink during colder months and its outdoor seating makes it a prime people-watching spot in summer.

Djuret

Lilla Nygata 5; tel: 08-506 400 84; www.djuret.se; Mon–Sat 5.30pm–midnight; $$$

The restaurant's name means 'animal'. The concept here is to serve one animal at a time, in its various cuts, then change the menu to accommodate another meat and is devised to encourage sustainability.

Fem Små Hus

Nygränd 10; tel: 08-10 87 75; www.femsmahus.se; Sun–Tue 5–11pm, Wed–Sat 5pm–midnight, $$$

Famed for both its cooking and atmosphere, situated in the cellar vaults of a hotel of the same name. Beautifully prepared dishes include platters of herring and reindeer cooked in port wine sauce.

The Flying Elk

Mälartorget 15; tel: 08-20 85 83; www.theflyingelk.se; Mon–Fri 5pm–midnight, Sat–Sun noon–midnight; $$

Busy gastropub in the heart of the Old Town boasting an outstanding list of bottled and tap beer. The food is of a good standard, too.

Kryp In

Prästgatan 17; tel: 08-20 88 41; www.restaurangkrypin.nu; Mon–Fri 5–11pm, Sat 12.30–11pm; $$

Tucked away on a quiet side street, this is a small but charming restaurant where you will find a good selection of attractive and tasty Nordic dishes.

Mälardrottningen

Riddarholmskajen 4; tel: 08-120 900 00; www.malardrottningen.se; Tue–Fri 6pm–midnight; $$

Once the American socialite Barbara Hutton's luxury yacht, now a restaurant permanently docked on the Riddarholmen quayside serving International and Swedish cuisine. Enjoy dining on the open deck with views over the water.

Reisen Bar offers a wide selection of spirits and a quirky menu

Mårten Trotzig

Västerlånggatan 79; tel: 08-442 25 30; www.martentrotzig.se; Mon–Fri 5pm–midnight, Sat–Sun noon–midnight; $$$

This fine-dining establishment consists of several dining rooms set around the courtyard of a historic building. Its menu is a great introduction to old Swedish favourites like meatballs served with mash and pickled cucumber.

Pubologi

Stora Nygatan 20; tel: 08-506 400 86; www.pubologi.se; Mon–Sat 5–10pm; $$$

Seeks inspiration from the Swedish countryside, offering such delights as duck liver with sweet cicely, or langoustine with ceps and rosehips. It has one of the largest wine cellars in Sweden, and brews its own unique beers.

Reisen Bar & Matsal

Skeppsbron 12; tel: 08-545 139 91; www.firsthotels.com; Mon–Fri 11.30am–2pm, 4pm–midnight, Sat 4pm–1am, Sun 5–11pm; $$$

Found within the First Hotel Reisen, the setting in this old building is quirky and offers delightful views over the water. The menu here is traditional with international influences.

Le Rouge

Brunnsgränd 24; tel: 08-505 244 30; www.lerouge.se; Tue 5–11pm, Wed–Thu 5pm–midnight, Fri–Sat 5pm–1am; $$$

In the cellars of a historic building this spectacular dining room serves high-end French cuisine with an Italian twist.

Siam

Stora Nygatan 25; tel: 08-20 02 33; www.siamrestaurant.se; Mon–Fri 11am–11pm, Sat noon–11pm, Sun 5–10pm; $$$

Underground Thai restaurant set in 17th-century cellars where spicy authentic food is served in generous portions.

Stadshuskällaren

Stadshuset; tel: 08-586 218 30; www.stadshuskallarensthlm.se; Mon–Tue 11.30am–2.30pm, Wed–Fri 11.30am–2.30pm, 5–11pm, Sat 5–11pm; $$$

Found in the basement of City Hall, serving contemporary Swedish cuisine in a beautiful setting which blends both old and new. Excellent service.

Modern City Centre

Browallshof

Surbrunnsgatan 20; tel: 08-16 51 36; www.browallshof.se; Mon–Fri 11.30am–11pm, Sat 5–11pm; $$$

This romantic inn has been serving superbly prepared classic fare since 1731. Highlights on the great Swedish-inspired menu are the seafood dishes.

Grill

Drottninggatan 89; tel: 08-31 45 30; www.grill.se; Mon–Fri 11am–1.30pm, 5pm–1am, Sat 4pm–1am; $$$

Here you can choose from five types of grill – *forno al legno* (brick oven), barbecue, charcoal, rotisserie and ishiyak – with some dishes cooked at your table.

Gourmet seafood at Stadshuskallaren

Kungshallen

Kungsgatan 44; www.kungshallen.eu; Mon–Fri 9am–11pm, Sat–Sun 11am–11pm; $

Near Hötorget in a historic building, this large food hall has 16 ethnic restaurants, so there's bound to be something here to suit everyone.

Mother

Mäster Samuelsgatan 19; tel: 08-505 244 39; www.motherstockholm.se; Mon–Sat 11.30am–1.30pm, 5–11pm, Sun brunch 11.30am–4pm; $$

A holistic dining experience where the food is created to please both your palate and your wellbeing. The aim is to feel that your body has been provided with well-balanced nutritious food, created with sustainability in mind.

Niklas

Regeringsgatan 66; tel: 08-20 60 10; www.niklas.se; Mon–Fri 1–11pm (Wed–Fri until 2am), Sat 5pm–2am; $$$

This trendy restaurant and bar is the baby of Swedish TV chef, Niklas Ekstedt. It serves Scandinavian and European dishes, all elegantly prepared in excellent, contemporary surroudings.

Smak

Oxtorgsgatan 14; tel: 08-22 09 52; www.restaurangentm.com; Mon–Fri 11.30am–2pm, 5–midnight (Fri until 2am), Sat 5pm–1am; $$$

Smak makes its guests pick three, five or seven flavours (for example, horse-radish, saffron, sesame, truffle, ginger, lemon, basil, tarragon), and then serves up tapas-sized dishes based around those tastes; the food is outstanding.

Storstad

Odengatan 41; tel: 08-673 38 00; www.storstad.se; Mon–Sat 4pm–1am; $$

This is the place to be seen, with a minimalist decor and crowded bar. The inventive French-Swedish food and courteous staff make it well worth a visit.

Tranan

Karlsbergsvägen 14; tel: 08-527 281 00; Mon–Fri 11.30am–11pm, Sat–Sun noon–11pm; $$$

In business since 1929, this bistro-style restaurant serves reliable international cuisine and excellent Swedish home cooking – the meatballs are delicious.

Victoria

Kungsträdgården 6; tel: 08-21 86 00; www.vickan.nu; Mon–Fri 11.30pm–3am (Tue–Thu until 11.30pm), Sat noon–3am; $$

A good value option considering the location. Try classic Swedish meatballs or the delicious fish and seafood casserole. There are plenty of outside tables from which to soak up the lively atmosphere.

Waipo

Drottninggatan 25; tel: 08-21 13 01; www.waipo.se; Mon–Fri 11am–10pm, Sat–Sun noon–10pm; $$

Waipo means grandma in Chinese, and the food here is suitably homely. All the

Fresh, Swedish fare at Mathias Dahlgren

authentic Chinese dishes are served in tasting portions so you can try as many dishes as possible.

Blasieholmen and Skeppsholmen

Bakfickan

Operahuset, Karl XII:S Torg; tel: 08-676 58 00; www.operakallaren.se; Mon–Fri 11.30am–11pm, Sat noon–10pm, Sun noon–5pm; $$$

This little restaurant is a real gem, attracting regular customers, including artists from the Opera House. The speciality of the 'Hip Pocket' is Swedish home cooking served over the bar counter.

B.A.R.

Blasieholmen 4a; tel: 08-611 53 35; www.restaurangbar.se; Mon–Fri 11.30pm–2am, 5pm–1am, Sat 4pm–1am; $$$

Participate in the creation of your meal by stepping up to the fish tank or ice counter to choose from a wide variety of fresh fish, meat, seafood, seasonal vegetables and condiments, and then watch as it is cooked to perfection.

Berns Asiatiska

Berzeli Park; tel: 08-566 327 67; www.berns.se; daily 6.30–10am, 11.30am–3pm, 7.30–11pm; $$$

Opened in 1863, this was a renowned restaurant and cabaret spot for over 100 years. Redesigned by Terence Conran, it is now a delightful bar-restaurant serving the best of modern Asian cuisine and also has a terrace.

Hjerta Skeppsholmen

Slupskjulsvägen 28; tel: 08-520 236 70; www.restauranghjerta.se; daily 11.30am–11pm; $$$

A feel of a seaside tavern – the restaurant is located on Skeppsholmen right beside the water with a rustic seating area outside. The Swedish- and French-inspired meals come with lots of fresh vegetables; try the Arichipelago box with different kinds of smoked and marinated fish.

Mathias Dahlgren

Södra Blasieholmshamnen 6; tel: 08-679 35 84; www.mathiasdahlgren.com; Mon–Sat 5pm–midnight; $$$$

Renowned chef Mathias Dahlgren uses the best Swedish ingredients to create elegant, unusual, melt-in-the-mouth dishes in his two Michelin-star restaurants at the Grand Hotel – Matbaren and Rutabaga (vegetarian). The superb food is complemented with exceptional wines, many of which are served by the glass.

Operabaren

Operahuset, Karl X11:s Torg; tel: 08-676 58 00; www.operakallaren.se; Mon–Wed 11.30am–11pm, Thu–Fri 11.30am–1am, Sat 12.30pm–1am; $$$

This has been a meeting place for Stockholm's artistic elite ever since it opened in 1905. The Art Deco interior, with comfortable leather armchairs and marble-topped tables, is a delightful setting for home-cooked Swedish dishes and the perfect setting for a pre-opera dinner and drinks.

Sample the traditional smorgasbord at The Veranda

Operakällarens Matsal

Operahuset, Karl XII:s Torg; tel: 08-676 58 01; www.operakallaren.se; Tue–Sat 6–10pm; $$$$

Dating back some 200 years, with a dining room considered the most beautiful in Sweden – enormous chandeliers, oil paintings and oak-panelled walls. It has a magnificent wine cellar, one of the best-stocked in the country, while pike, char and langoustine are highlights of the one Michelin star menu.

The Veranda

Södra Blaiseholmshamnen 8; tel: 08-679 35 86; www.grandhotel.se/en; Mon–Fri 7–10.30am, 11.30am–11pm, Sat–Sun 7–11am, noon–11pm; $$$

No one should leave Stockholm without trying a *smörgåsbord* at this delightful restaurant in the Grand Hôtel, which looks out over the Royal Palace across the water. A small bottle of the house special, 1874 Grand Aquavit, comes with the meal.

Wedholms Fisk

Nybrokajen 17; tel: 08-611 78 74; www.wedholmsfisk.se; Mon–Fri 11.30am–11pm, Sat 5–11pm; $$$

Seafood lovers, this is the place for you. All the ingredients are carefully selected and prepared according to the classic Swedish and French standards. The sauces are excellent, the portions are generous, and the decor sober. Come here for lunch and you'll get good value for your money.

Djurgården

Flickorna Helin Voltaire

Rosendalsvägen 14; tel: 08-664 51 08; www.helinvoltaire.com; Mon–Sat 9am–5pm, $

Housed in a twisty, 'fairy-tale castle' on Djurgården, this is the place for coffee and cake in high summer, or hot chocolate in front of a roaring fire in winter.

Oaxen Krog

Beckholmsvagen 26; tel: 08-551 531 05; www.oaxen.com; Tue–Sat 6–10pm; $$$$

Diners are led through a secret door into an oak-furnished dining room. Expertly crafted by chef Magnus Ek, you can choose from the 6- or 10-course menu which in true New Nordic style, makes the most of local, seasonal ingredients. Two Michelin stars.

Spritmuseums Restaurang

Djurgårdsvågen 38; tel: 08-121 313 00; www.spritmuseum.se; daily noon–2.30pm (Sat–Sun until 3pm), also Tue–Sat 6–10pm; $$

Head chef Petter Nilsson uses carefully sourced local produce in this creative kitchen. Round off a dish of braised lamb with a dessert of mandarin sorbet and liquorice meringue.

Östermalm

The Bull and Bear Inn

Birger Jalsgatan 16; tel: 08-611 10 00; www.bullandbear.se; Mon–Thu 3pm–3am, Fri 2pm–3am, Sat 1pm–3am, Sun 1pm–midnight; $$

Probably Stockholm's most authentic English pub, serving typical pub food

Michelin-starred, conceptual dining at Oaxen Krog

combined with a huge selection of draught and bottled beers and over 200 types of malt whisky.

Cassi

Narvavagen 30; tel: 08-661 74 61; www.cassi.se; Mon–Fri 10.45am–8pm, Sun 1–8pm; $$$

Eat modern European cuisine at this pleasant bistro-style restaurant with a friendly atmosphere. Expertly grilled meats are accompanied by their legendary Béarnaise sauce and amazing French fries. The largely French wine list is heavy on reds and whites.

Eriks Bakficka

Fredrikshovsgatan 4; tel: 08-660 15 99; www.eriks.se; Mon–Fri 11.30am–2.30pm, 5–10pm (Fri 4.30–11pm), Sat 5–11pm; $$$

A stone's throw from the Djurgården bridge, this charming, reliable restaurant doesn't look much from the outside but delivers delicious modern, Swedish cuisine inside. Famous for its delicious desserts.

Halv Grek Plus Turk

Jungfrugatan 33; tel: 08-665 94 22; www.halv grekplusturk.se; Mon–Fri 11.30am–2pm, 5pm–10pm, Sat–Sun dinner only; $

This restaurant is situated on a quiet corner in Östermalm and offers excellent value dishes from the eastern Mediterranean region, notably Greece and Turkey. The generous meze dishes come highly recommended and are also outstanding value.

PA & Co

Riddargatan 8; tel: 08-611 08 45; www.paco.se; daily 5pm–midnight; $$

This well-known restaurant, with excellent French-influenced food, has been a locals' favourite for over 20 years so it can be hard to get a table.

Restaurant at The Diplomat

Strandvägen 7C; tel: 08-459 68 02; www.diplomathotel.com; Mon–Fri 7.30–10am, 11.30am–2.30pm, 5–10pm, Sat–Sun brunch 1–4pm; $$$

Modern and stylish, this restaurant is located on the ground floor of the Hotel Diplomat with views over the water from huge picture windows. The menu focuses on traditional Swedish fare with Mediterranean touches.

Sturehof

Stureplan 2; tel: 08-440 57 30; www.sturehof.com; Mon–Fri 11am–2pm, 7.30–midnight, Sat–Sun 11am–2pm; $$$

A restaurant and bar situated at the centre of the city's nightlife; the food is good, reliable Swedish fare. This is not the main reason why people flock here, they come for the Jonas Bohlin-designed interior, the lively bar and the excellent company.

Södermalm

Chutney

Katarina Bangata 19; tel: 08-640 30 10; www.chutney.se; Mon–Fri 11am–midnight, Sat noon–10pm, Sun noon–9pm; $

Here you'll find delicious vegetarian food for a surprisingly reasonable price. Chut-

Industrial chic at LUX Dag för Dag

ney is a relaxed, hipster-style place – as you'd expect in bohemian Södermalm – with a café atmosphere. Pay for a tasty main then help yourself to bread, salad and pomegranate-flavoured water from the buffet table.

La Cucaracha

Bondegatan 2; tel: 08-644 39 44; www.lacucaracha.se; daily 5–11pm (Wed, Thu until midnight; Fri, Sat until 1am); $$

Tucked away, this fine, authentic Spanish restaurant has an enticing selection of tapas, single or combination plates, desserts, wines and beers.

Gondolen

Stadsgården 6; tel: 08-641 70 90; www.erik.se; Mon 11.30am–11pm, Tue–Sat 11.30am–1am; $$$

Eating here is a real Stockholm experience. Gondolen, regarded by Stockholmers as an institution, offers excellent traditional Swedish cuisine with a great view over the city. Those on a tighter budget can enjoy the same view at the bar.

Pelikan

Blekingegatan 40; tel: 08-556 090 90; www.pelikan.se; Mon–Thu 4pm–midnight, Fri–Sun noon–1am; $$$

Over 100 years of dining memories hover beneath the ceiling paintings in this traditional beer hall. Meatballs, herring and reindeer are some of the favourites, as is the knuckle of pork, gently cooked overnight and served with mashed swede.

Further Afield

Döden I Grytan

Norrtullsgatan 61; tel: 08-32 50 95; www.dodenigrytan.se; daily 5.30pm–midnight (Sun until 10pm); $$

New Nordic cuisine may be all the rage, but this restaurant in a traditional Swedish tavern close to Hagaparken specialises in refreshingly authentic Italian fare (enormous portions!). The atmosphere is rustic and romantic.

Dryck

Olof Palmes plats 2, Uppsala; tel: 703 123 556; www.dryckuppsala.se; Tue–Sat from 5pm; $$$

This tiny place, which feels more like a private kitchen than a restaurant, starts with a novel idea – choose the wine first, then cook the food to fit. The result is an outstanding menu that puts Dryck head and shoulders above anywhere else in Uppsala. A must visit if you are planning a day trip to Uppsala. Book to avoid disappointment.

Lux Dag för Dag

Primusgatan 116; tel: 08-619 01 90; www.luxdagfordag.se; Tue–Fri 11.30am–2pm, 5–11pm, Sat 5–11pm; $$$

This restaurant found on one of the smaller islands is worth the short taxi ride from the city centre. Housed in the old Electrolux factory building that has been transformed into a beautiful example of Scandinavian design, the specialities are modern, innovative dishes based on home-grown traditions.

Take in the original surroundings at Drottningholms Slottsteater

NIGHTLIFE

This is just a selection of the key or landmark venues of Stockholm's vibrant nightlife scene. Tickets for an event can often be bought at the ticket office of the relevant venue. You can also book in advance with the help of your hotel, the Stockholm Visitor Centre at Kulturhuset, Sergels Torg 5, or at a ticket agency (for a fee) such as www.ticketmaster.se.

Classical Music

Berwaldhallen
Dag Hammarskjölds väg 3; tel: 08-784 18 00; www.berwaldhallen.se
World-class classical music is played here regularly by the Swedish Radio Symphony Orchestra, the Swedish National Radio Chorus and guest orchestras.

Konserthuset
Hörtorget 8; tel: 08-506 677 88; www.konserthuset.se
Home of the Royal Philharmonic Orchestra, an internationally acclaimed 100-piece orchestra currently led by American conductor Alan Gilbert, whose season runs from September to May or June.

Opera, Theatre and Dance

Confidencen
Ulriksdals Slottsteater; tel: 08-85 70 16; www.confidencen.se
Sweden's oldest rococco theatre stages weekly opera and ballet at Ulriksdal Slott (Castle) June to September.

Dansens Hus
Barnhusgatan 12–14; tel: 08-508 990 90; www.dansenshus.se
The largest dance stage in northern Europe. Many established companies make guest appearances here.

Drottningholm Slottsteater
Drottningholm Palace; tel: 08-556 931 00; www.dtm.se
In summer, this unusual 18th-century theatre hosts major operas, using the original stage settings and machinery.

Kungliga Dramatiska Teatren
Nybroplan; tel: 08-667 06 80; www.dramaten.se
This most prestigious five-stage theatre hosts modern and classical plays.

Kungliga Operan
Gustav Adolfs Torg; tel: 08-791 44 00; www.operan.se
This 100-year-old theatre hosts international opera productions from mid-August to June as well as top-class classical ballet such as Swan Lake, The Nutcracker and Romeo and Juliet.

Stockholm Stadsteater
Sergels Torg; tel: 08-506 201 00; www.stadsteatern.stockholm.se
Housed inside the Kulturhuset (see page 39), the main auditorium stages a varied musical programme.

The ambient atmosphere at the Stora Salongen at Berns

Bars, Clubs and Live Music

Absolut Icebar

Vasaplan 4; tel: 08-505 635 20; www.icebarstockholm.se

The world's first permanent ice bar. It may be a little gimmicky, but it's fun for a quick cocktail. Reservations required.

Berns

Berzelli Park 6; tel: 08-566 322 00; www.berns.se

This entertainment palace at Berzelli Park has been in existence since 1863 and was redesigned a few years ago. It now has several stylish bars and attracts a trendy crowd.

Café Opera

Operahuset, Kungsträdgården; tel: 08-676 58 07; www.cafeopera.se

Expensive but ever-popular bar, this restaurant and club attracts a mix of people in a venue dating from 1895.

Fasching Jazzclubb

Kungsgatan 63; tel: 08-20 00 06; www.fasching.se

Stockholm's largest and most popular club for jazz, with a restaurant and nightclub, too. There are performances nearly every day of the week.

Nalen

Regeringsgatan 74; tel: 08-505 292 00; www.nalen.com

An illustrious 1950s ballroom that is undergoing a revival as a restaurant, bar and concert venue.

Patricia

Söder Mälarstrand, Kajplats 19; tel: 08-743 05 70; www.patricia.st

This steamship saw active service in WWII, but today it is a fun-time party boat, with three floors of bars.

Rose

Hamngatan 2; tel: 08-440 56 30; www.roseclub.se

A relative newcomer but already one of the city's hottest nightclubs, this decadent EDM (electronic dance music) nightclub is all velvet and gold.

Sky Bar

Vasagatan 1; tel: 08-506 540 37; www.skybarstockholm.se

While sipping a cocktail, the view after dark through floor-to-ceiling glass is amazing at this sleek bar on the ninth floor of the Royal Viking Hotel.

Spy Bar

Birger Jarlsgatan 2l; tel: 08-545 076 55; www.stureplansgruppen.se

One of Stockholm's most legendary bar/nightclubs, Spy Bar is popular with an intellectual, 'hipster' crowd. The dress code is smart casual.

Sturecompagniet

Sturegatan 4; tel: 08-545 076 00; www.sturecompagniet.se

A favourite with local soap stars and the young and trendy, this massive club sprawling across three floors features a dramatic ballroom entrance.

Blue and yellow flags fly during the annual National Day celebrations

A–Z

A

Age restrictions

Wines, spirits and beers above 3.5 per cent can only be purchased from shops run by the *Systembolaget* (alcohol monopoly; see page 19). The legal minimum age for buying alcohol in these shops is 20 (you may be asked for ID), though in restaurants and bars the legal age is 18. Some clubs impose a minimum age for entry of up to 26 for men and 24 for women.

In order to rent a vehicle in Sweden you must be at least 18 years old, however the minimum age may vary depending on car category, and you must have held a driver's license for at least one year.

B

Budgeting

The following are some approximate prices in Swedish kronor (kr) to help you plan your travelling budget:

Hotels: A double room with a shared bathroom in a cheap hotel costs around 800kr. A double in a moderate hotel is around 1,500kr, and a deluxe double anything from 2,000 to 3,000kr depending on the establishment.

Drinks: In a restaurant a glass of beer or house wine costs around 70 to 80kr.

Food: For a main course, expect to pay 70 to 90kr at a budget, 150 to 200kr at a moderate and anything from 300kr upwards at an expensive restaurant.

Transport: A single pre-paid transport ticket in Stockholm costs 43kr. The taxi journey from airport to Stockholm should cost 500 to 550kr, depending on the company and whether or not you have pre-booked.

C

Children

Stockholm is very child-friendly. Swedes are good at devising attractions for the whole family, and there are some excellent amusement parks, water parks and zoos. Museums are usually free to those aged 18 and under, and many have a hands-on section aimed at children. Many toilets in the city have changing facilities and most major hotels in Stockholm offer a babysitting service.

The city's public transport system and other amenities were created with families in mind. Navigating a pushchair in Stockholm is no problem as there are ramps leading down to subway stations and city buses automatically lower a platform in the rear to admit pushchairs and prams. On all public transport in Stockholm, children under 7 years of age travel free, while children between 7 and 19 pay about half price when accompanied by a paying adult.

If visiting in winter be prepared for cold weather and snow

Clothing

Although the weather is usually very pleasant during the day in the short summer months, it cools enough at night to make a sweater or light jacket necessary. The weather can be unpredictable, so pack a light waterproof coat. In the spring and autumn thicker clothing will be required, while in winter warm boots, coat, hat, gloves and scarf are necessary. Stockholmers do not dress up and even at the theatre or opera smart casual clothes are the norm.

Crime and safety

Sweden is one of the safest countries in the world, however there are warnings in hotels advising visitors not to leave bags unattended. This, obviously, is good policy anywhere and it is also good policy to check your valuables – including passport and airline tickets – into the hotel safe. Another sensible precaution is to take photocopies of passports and airline tickets and keep them separate from the originals. In instances where the originals are lost this will save an enormous amount of hassle.

Any loss or theft should be reported at once to the nearest police station, if only for insurance purposes.

In 2017, it was Stockholm's turn to be the target of a terrorist attack, when a truck ploughed into a busy department store killing 4 people and injuring many others. As for other European capitals, vigilance is key.

Customs

There are no restrictions on importing/exporting goods for people travelling between Sweden and other EU countries, as long as the goods are for personal use and not resale; guide levels are 3,200 cigarettes, 400 cigarillos, 200 cigars, 1kg tobacco, 10 litres of spirits, 20 litres of fortified wine, 90 litres of wine and 110 litres of beer. Visitors travelling to/from non-EU countries can import duty-free 200 cigarettes/100 cigarillos/50 cigars or 250g tobacco, 1 litre of spirits or 2 litres of dessert wine (maximum 22 percent alcohol by volume), 4 litres of wine plus 16 litres of beer. You must be at least 18 years old to bring in tobacco, and at least 20 to bring in alcohol. All travellers entering or leaving the EU with €10,000 or more in cash must declare the sum to Customs.

Disabled travellers

Many hotel rooms and facilities are adapted for the needs of people with mobility problems. New public buildings and most public toilets are wheelchair-accessible. Most buses have easy access for people with wheelchairs. Mainline and underground trains have elevators or ramps.

To get a guide to Swedish restaurants with disabled access contact DHR De Handikappades Riksförbund (tel: 08-685 80 00; www.dhr.se)

Drottninggattan is one of central Stockholm's busiest shopping streets

E

Electricity

The normal electric current in Sweden is 220 volts AC 50 Hz. Sweden uses the Europlug (Type C & F) for electricity, with two round prongs. Travellers should plan for adapters and/or transformers.

Embassies and consulates

Embassies and consulates in Stockholm:
Australia: Klarabergsviadukten 63, 8th Floor; tel: 08-613 29 00; www.sweden. embassy.gov.au
Canada: Klarabergsgatan 23, 6th Floor; tel: 08-453 30 00; www.canadainter national.gc.ca
Ireland: Hovslagargatan 5; tel: 08-545 040 40; www.dfa.ie/irish-embassy/ sweden
UK: Skarpögatan 6–8; tel: 08-671 30 00; www.britishembassy.se
US: Dag Hammarskjölds Väg 31; tel: 08-783 53 00; www.usemb.se

Emergencies

The emergency telephone number for police, fire and ambulance is 112. It can be dialled free of charge from all public telephones, but should only be used in case of emergency. Call 114 114 for non-urgent police assistance.

Etiquette

Swedes are meticulously polite to foreigners. Punctuality is vital – always call and apologise if you are going to be late.

Many shops and offices have a ticket machine somewhere on the premises. To be served, take a ticket and then wait for your number to be shown on the display.

G

Gay/lesbian travellers

Sweden is renowned for its liberal attitudes to sex, and its age of consent is 15 for heterosexuals and gays. Same-sex marriages have been legal in Sweden since 2009. But nevertheless the gay scene in Stockholm is less apparent than in other capitals, although there are a few of men-only, women-only and mixed gay clubs.

Information and advice can be obtained from the Stockholms Gay Centre (Sveavägen 59, tel: 08-501 62 900; www.rfsl.se). QX is an LGBT magazine that offers the most up-to-date information about clubs, restaurants, bars and shops in Stockholm and elsewhere (www.qx.se).

H

Health

No vaccinations are needed for entry to Sweden. EU residents should obtain the European Health Insurance Card (EHIC), which entitles them to emergency medical and hospital treatment (available in the UK free online at www.ehic.org.uk or by phoning 0300 330 1350). Citizens of non-EU countries should ensure they have adequate travel/health insurance.

The independent boutiques of Gamla Stan are perfect for a spot of souvenir shopping

If you are in need of a doctor, call or go to CityAkuten, Apelbergsgatan 48, tel: 010-601 00 00; www.cityakuten.se; Mon–Fri 8.30am–4.30pm). There is also a 24-hour non-emergency health helpline, tel: 1177.

Several city hospitals have accident and emergency clinics. These include Karolinska Sjukhuset (Karolinska Vägen, tel: 08-517 700 00, 24-hour); Södersjukhuset (Sjukhusbacken 10, tel: 08-616 10 00); Capio Sankt Görans (Sankt Göransplan 1, tel: 08-587 010 00); St Eriks Sjukhus (for optical and dental emergencies, tel: 08-545 512 20). Take your passport with you for identification

Pharmacies *(apoteket)* can dispense medicines for most minor ailments without a prescription, and the staff can usually advise on appropriate medication. Pharmacies are normally open Mon–Fri 10–4 or 6pm, and some also open on Sat. A 24-hour pharmacy service is offered by C.W. Scheele (Klarabergsgatan 64), near the Central Station. Nevertheless, it is a good idea to bring along an adequate supply of any prescribed medication from home.

I

Internet facilities

Most airports, train stations, public libraries and hotels throughout Sweden have free Wi-Fi or computers with internet access. There are also plenty of cafés with Wi-Fi or internet terminals in Stockholm. Branches of the coffee chain Espresso House offer free WiFi.

M

Media

Newspapers and magazines: Sweden's main daily newspapers are *Svenska Dagbladet*, *Dagens Nyheter*, *Göteborgs Posten*, *Expressen* and *Aftonbladet*. English-language newspapers and a variety of magazines are available at kiosks and tobacco shops in Stockholm, usually on the day of publication.

Radio: Radio Sweden (Sveriges Radio) broadcasts news and information in English, which can be heard in the Stockholm area on FM 89.6 MHz. Check the Radio Sweden website: www.sverigesradio.se. BBC World Service programmes are also available on channel 89.6 FM.

Television: All foreign programs on Swedish TV are shown in the original language with Swedish subtitles. Sweden's state-run STV1 and STV2, and the commercial TV4, show English-language films, chat shows, sport, movies and soap operas.

Money

Currency: Sweden's currency is the krona (plural kronor), abbreviated to sek, kr, and divided into 100 öre. Denominations come in 1, 2, 5 and 10 kronor coins. Banknotes are available in 20, 50, 100, 200, 500 and 1,000 kronor. As Sweden remains outside the European

There are many outdoor markets to explore, especially in the summer months

Monetary Union (EMU), the Euro is not used (with exceptions).

Currency exchange: Foreign currency can be changed in all commercial and savings banks as well as in the larger hotels and department stores. FOREX (www.forex.se) has offices at Central-stationen (Central Station), Arlanda Airport and throughout the city that are open daily.

Credit cards and travellers' cheques: Leading credit cards are accepted almost everywhere throughout the city. You can draw cash out using a Visa, MasterCard, Maestro or Cirrus card in any "Bankomat" or "Uttagsautomat" ATMs. Travellers' cheques can be exchanged without difficulty at all banks.

Taxes: Value Added Tax (called 'Moms' in Sweden) is included in the sales price of goods, and is 25 percent except on food, which is 12 percent. Up to 19 percent refund is available to non-EU residents on products valued at more than 200kr in shops displaying the Tax Free Shopping sign. When paying for your purchases, ask the shop staff for a Tax Free Form and to seal your bag as proof you haven't used the item. The refund is made at the airport on departure, at Stockholm Arlanda Terminal 5. For further details see www.globalblue.com.

Tipping: In hotels and restaurants a service charge is included in the bill and a further tip is not expected. Taxi drivers are usually tipped. Cloakrooms at restaurants and clubs charge about 15–20kr. Tipping for special services provided by hotel staff is fine but not expected.

Opening hours

Shopping hours are generally 9.30am–6/7pm weekdays and 10am–4/5pm on Saturday; department stores may remain open until 8pm or 9pm; chains and several notable shops in the city centre are open on Sunday 11am until 3/4pm. Most museums and other attractions are generally open either from 10am to 5pm or from 11am to 6pm, although there are longer opening hours during the summer season. Some close on Mondays and some over the winter. Banks generally open Mon–Fri 9.30–3pm (some 6pm) and close on Saturday and Sunday).

Banks, offices and shops close on public holidays in Sweden, as do most restaurants and many museums and tourist attractions.

Public Holidays
1 January New Year's Day
6 January Epiphany
March/April Good Friday and Easter Monday
1 May Labour Day
May Ascension (usually second part of the month); Pentecost (10 days after Ascension)
6 June National Day
June Midsummer's Eve (around the 24th)

November All Saints' Day (usually at start of the month)
25 and 26 December Christmas
31 December New Year's Eve

P

Post

Fanchised postal kiosks are located in grocery stores, such as Hemköp in the basement of the Åhléns City at Sergels Torg. You can purchase stamps at Pressbyrån kiosks, bookstalls and stationers' shops. Letters and postcards of up to 20 grams cost 6kr within Sweden and 12kr internationally. Post boxes are painted different colours: yellow boxes are for mail to destinations abroad and the rest of Sweden; blue boxes for letters within the Stockholm area. For more information, visit www.posten.se.

R

Religion

The Swedish State Church is in the Lutheran tradition. Stockholm has a wide range of places of worship, including a Greek Orthodox church, several synagogues and mosques.

S

Smoking

Smoking is not allowed in public spaces, which includes bars, restaurants and all forms of public transport.

T

Telephones

Most payphones no longer take coins – they operate only with credit cards (sign-posted CCC) or a telephone card *(telia telefonkort)*. Telephone cards are widely available in shops and kiosks. The telephone directory enquiry service is also expensive (tel: 118 118).

The Sweden country code is 46. The Stockholm area code is 08. To call abroad, dial 00 followed by the country code (44 for the UK, 1 for the US and Canada, 353 for Ireland, 61 for Australia and 64 for New Zealand), then dial the number, omitting any initial 0.

Swedish mobile phones operate on the 900/1800 MHz GSM network – most European phones are compatible, although your phone must be unlocked in order to link up with the network. US phones work on a slightly different frequency, so US visitors should check with their phone company first regarding usability. The cheapest way to use your own mobile phone is to buy a Swedish SIM card from a newsagent or telephone operator. Local mobile network operators include Tele2 (www.tele2.se), Telenor (www.telenor.se) and Telia (www.telia.se).

Time zones

Sweden conforms to Central European Time, which is one hour ahead of Greenwich Mean Time (GMT) and six hours

The Djurgården ferry runs regularly between Djurgården and Slussen

ahead of Eastern Standard Time (EST). In summer Sweden moves to daylight saving time from the last weekend in March to the last weekend in October, which means that it is one hour ahead of Central European Time.

Toilets

Public facilities are located in some underground stations, department stores and some of the bigger streets, squares and parks. Toilets are rarely free of charge. Some have slots for coins or an attendant to give towels and soap. The usual charge is 5kr.

Tourist information

The main tourist office, run by Stockholm Visitors Board (SVB), is the Stockholm Visitor Centre (Kulturhuset, Sergels Torg 3; tel: 08-508 285 08; www.visitstockholm.com; May–mid-Sept Mon–Fri 9am–7pm, Sat 9am–4pm, Sun 10am–4pm, Jan–Apr, mid-Sept–Dec Mon–Fri 9am–6pm, Sat 9am–4pm, Sun 10am–4pm), where you can acquire maps, books and other tourist information and have free Wi-Fi access. For general information about Sweden visit www.visitsweden.com.

Tours and guides

Guides: The Stockholm Tourist Service operates a private guide and group booking service (tel: 08-120 049 50; www.stotourist.se), and books transport and authorised guides for individuals and groups.

Boat tours: Strömma (tel: 08-120 040 00; www.stromma.se) offers several boat tours of the city and the archipelago.

Bus tours: Strömma also offer a variety of bus tours, including Stockholm Panorama, which lasts just 75 minutes, has multilingual commentary and departs from Gustav II Adolfs Torg.

On foot: Stockholm Our Way offers several interesting walking tours, the highlight of which is the Old Town Walk, as well as biking and boat trips (tel: 08-410 773 30; www.ourwaytours.com). Fans of Stieg Larsson's Millennium series should not miss the Millennium Tour following the footsteps of the books' main characters, Mikael Blomkvist and Lisbeth Salander (organised by the Stadsmuseet, Ryssgården, tel. 08-508 316 20; www.stadsmuseet.stockholm.se).

Balloon rides: Stockholm is one of the few world capitals in which you can fly in a hot-air balloon over the city centre. Contact Far & Flyg (tel: 70-340 41 07, www.farochflyg.se) to book.

Transport

Arrival

By air: The national carrier SAS Scandinavian Airlines (www.flysas.com) is part of the Star Alliance airline partnership. Stockholm's main international airport is Arlanda (www.swedavia.com/arlanda), 37km (23 miles) north of Stockholm but the city is also served by three other airports. Bromma (www.swedavia.se/bromma), 8km/5 miles northwest of Stockholm, is used mainly by smaller

Hot-air ballon ride over Riddarholms Church

domestic airlines. Budget airlines fly in to Skavsta (www.skavsta.se), 100km/62 miles southwest of Stockholm, and Västerås (www.vst.nu), 100km/62 miles west of Stockholm.

There are direct flights from many airports in the UK and Ireland to Stockholm. Scandinavian Airlines (SAS) and British Airways (www.britishairways.com) operate direct daily flights from London Heathrow to Stockholm Arlanda. Several budget carriers also make frequent flights to Stockholm. Ryanair (www.ryan air.com) operates flights from London Stansted to Stockholm's Västerås and Skavsta airports. Norwegian (www.norwe gian.com) flies direct daily to Stockholm Arlanda from London Stansted, and several times per week from Edinburgh and Manchester.

Services between Stockholm and North America are operated by SAS, in connection with United Airlines (www. united.com) and other Star Alliance members, with direct flights from Newark, NJ, Chicago and Los Angeles to Stockholm Arlanda. Delta Airlines (www.delta.com) have direct flights to Stockholm from New York, JFK.

From Arlanda airport, the shortest journey is by the Arlanda Express train (www. arlandaexpress.com), which operates four times an hour and costs 280kr each way (cheaper if bought in advance) for the 20-minute trip to Central Station. The Flygbussarna shuttle bus service (www. flygbussarna.se) operates between all of the airports and the City Terminal at Cen-

tral Station, and is the cheapest option. Costs and times vary depending on which airport you are travelling from but from Arlanda it costs about 120kr each way (215 return).

Taxis are always available but very expensive. Insist on the fixed charge rate (between 450–520kr to the city centre), which generally work out cheaper than a metered taxi ride, particularly during rush hour.

Several international car-hire companies have offices at Arlanda Airport and in Stockholm city centre, including Avis (tel: 0770 820 082; www.avis.se) and Hertz (tel: 0771 211 212; www.hertz.se). **By rail and coach:** Rail travel from much of Europe to Stockholm is quite quick, comfortable and inexpensive. Swedish State Railway (Statens Järnvägar or SJ; tel: Swedish 0771-75 75 75; www.sj.se) operate an efficient electrified network leaving Stockholm for most big towns every hour or two. The X2000 high-speed train, which can reach speeds of up to 200km/h (124mph), drastically cut the travelling times between Stockholm and other cities within the country. There are ticket machines at most stations, selling first and second class tickets.

The InterRail Sweden Pass (www.inter rail.eu) offers European travellers who live outside Sweden unlimited rail travel within Sweden for 3, 4, 6 or 8 days within any one month. Seats must be reserved in advance. The Eurail Sweden Pass (www.eurail.com) has similar terms, but is aimed at non-European travellers.

Stockholm is easy to explore by bike with cyclepaths throughout the city

Travelling by coach is usually cheap compared to rail but travelling time is longer. An efficient network of express coach services links many major towns and cities, operated mainly by Swebus Express (tel: 0771-218 218; www.swe bus.se), which covers most of the south and centre of the country, and runs as far north as Umeå.

By road: Visitors arriving in Sweden from Denmark can use the impressive Öresund toll bridge between Copenhagen and Malmö. On the Swedish side the E6 motorway connects to the E4 across the country to Stockholm. Speed limits on Swedish motorways are normally 110kmh (68mph) but 120kmh (75mph) on some; 90kmh (56mph) on other major roads. In densely populated areas the speed limit is 50–70kmh (30–42mph) and 40–60kmh (25–37mph) in some cities.

There are no direct ferry routes from the UK to Scandinavia but there are many links from other countries in Europe to Sweden, including Denmark, Estonia, Finland, Germany, Latvia, Lithuania, Norway and Poland.

Within Stockholm

Buses: Buses provide a pleasant and economical way to see the city. The local network in Stockholm is claimed to be the world's largest and is operated by the Stockholm Transit Authority (SL; www.sl.se), which also runs the underground and local mainline train services, trams and some of the ferry lines in Greater Stockholm. Red city buses operate on the inner-city routes while blue buses cover the routes out to the suburbs. The best sightseeing routes are 2, 3, 44, 65 and 69, which cover most of the central area and many sights.

Single journey tickets, valid for 75 minutes, cannot be bought with cash on the bus, but must be bought in advance at shops such as Pressbyrån that display the SL logo, SL travel centres or ticket offices and machines at Metro stations. You can buy a travel card, valid on all of SL's routes, that you keep topping up with cash (like London's Oyster card); or alternatively, you can buy 24-hour, 72-hour or 7-day travel cards, which allow you to travel freely across Stockholm during those time periods.

Underground: Stockholm is justifiably proud of its underground railway, known as T-banan (the T stands for tunnel – all stations are identified by the T sign). The T-banan is spotless, and more than 100 stations cover more than 95km (60 miles) over three routes – red, green and blue – that all link up to Central Station. Work on new extensions started in 2016; the plan is for an additional nine stations by 2025. It operates from 5am until 3.30am Sunday to Thursday and until 4am on Friday and Saturday.

Trams: The No 7 tram operates between Sergels Torg and Waldemarsudde on Djurgården using a regular SL ticket (every 15 minutes, Mon–Fri 6.30am–1am). A restored vintage tram also trundles along

Eclectic artwork in an underground station

the same route (Apr–Nov) but starting from Norrmalmstorg.

Boats: Stockholm and its environs are made-to-order for boat excursions and scheduled ferry services. Sightseeing boats cruise under the city's bridges, steamers serve the islands of the archipelago in the Baltic and ply the waters of Lake Mälaren. The most popular short-hop ferry trips are those from central Stockholm (Slussen) out to the island of Djurgården via Skeppsholmen, operated by Waxholmsbolaget (www.waxholms bolaget.se). An SL Card includes the ferries from Slussen and single tickets can be bought at the kiosk on the quayside. Strömma (www.stromma.se) operates cruises in the Stockholm archipelago.

Bicycle: Stockholm has a public bike scheme operating Apr–Oct 6am–10pm, although you can return bikes up to 1am. You can borrow and drop off bikes at some 140 stands throughout the city by buying a three-day cycle card, available at various hotels, hostels, travel centres and newsagents' kiosks (tel: 077 444 24 24; www.citybikes.se). The card can also be used to borrow bicycles from four stands in Uppsala.

Taxis: There are plenty of taxis available and you can flag them down anywhere in Stockholm if the sign on the roof is illuminated. Find them at stands marked 'Taxi', or call them by telephone. Taxi Stockholm (www.taxistockholm.se; tel: 08-15 00 00) is a well-known firm. Be cautious: Sweden does not regulate taxi prices and they vary greatly. Check the highest unit price

(usually 290–390kr) on the yellow sticker that is usually displayed on the rear door window before entering the taxi. The price is based on a 10km, 15-minute journey.

Visas and passports

A valid passport entitles you to stay for up to three months, and visas are not normally required. Passports are not required by visitors from EU countries, only an identity card. A valid passport entitles EU and North American visitors to stay for a maximum of 90 days, and visas are not normally required. Sweden is part of the Schengen Area, and citizens of other Schengen countries should be allowed to enter without passports and if you arrive from another Scandinavian country, passports aren't usually checked at all. However, in January 2016 Sweden introduced identity checks for travellers from Denmark in an attempt to reduce the number of migrants arriving in the country. If you intend to stay longer than 90 days, you will need to obtain a resident's permit, which you can do once you are in Sweden. See www.migrationsverket.se for further information.

Weights and measures

Sweden uses the metric system. Beware of the Swedish word mil, which is sometimes translated erroneously as "mile" – it actually means 10km (6.2 miles).

ÅHLÉNS CITY

A Swedish shopping institution, Åhléns department store

LANGUAGE

The Alphabet

The Swedish alphabet has 29 letters; the additional three are å, ä and ö and come after the letter Z. To find Mr Åkerblad in the phone book, therefore, look at the end of the listings. (Note that the index in this guide uses the English A to Z alphabet.)

Greetings

Yes *Ja*
No *Nej*
Hello *Hej*
Goodbye *Hejdå*
Thank you *Tack*
Please *Tack/Var så god*
Do you speak English? *talar du engelska?*
Today *Idag*
Tomorrow *I morgon*
Yesterday *I går*
What time is it? *Hur mycket är klockan?*
It is (the time is) *Den är (klockan är)*
My name is *Jag heter*
Can I help you? *Kan jag hjälpa till?*
I do not understand *Jag förstår inte*
I do not know *Jag vet inte*

Eating and Drinking

breakfast *Frukost*
lunch *Lunch*
dinner *Middag*
eat *Äta*
drink *Dricka*
cheers *Skål!*

Menu Decoder

starters *förrätter*
main courses *huvudrätter, varmrätter*
desserts *desserter*
drink *dryck*
bröd **bread**
fisk **fish**
fläsk **pork**
grillad **grilled**
grädde **cream**
grönsaker **vegetables**
helstekt **roast**
hummer **lobster**
jordgubbar **strawberries**
kalkon **turkey**
kalv **veal**
kyckling **chicken**
kött **meat**
köttbullar **meatballs**
lax **salmon**
lök **onion**
mjölk **milk**
morötter **carrots**
ost **cheese**
ostron **oysters**
potatis **potato**
ris **rice**
räkor **prawns**
rökt **smoked**
smör **butter**
smörgås **sandwich**
soppa **soup**
stekt **fried**
tårta **cake**
öl **beer**

Organic, healthy food is easy to find in Stockholm

Accommodation

to rent *att hyra*
chalet *stuga*
sauna *bastu*
launderette *tvättomat*
dry cleaning *kemtvätt*
dirty *smutsigt*
clean *ren*

On the Road

How do I get to? *Hur kommer jag till?*
Where is …? *Var finns…?*
Right *Höger*
To the right *Till höger*
Left *Vänster*
To the left *Till vänster*
Straight on *Rakt fram*

Shopping

open *öppen/öppet*
closed *stängt*
to buy *att köpa*
department store *varuhus*
food *mat*
money *pengar*
shop *affär*
How much is this? *Vad kostar det?*
It costs *Det kostar*
Do you have English newspapers? *Har du engelska tidningar?*

Health & Emergencies

chemist/pharmacy *apotek*
accident & emergency clinic *akutmottagning/vårdcentral*
hospital *sjukhus*
doctor *doktor*
police station *polisstation*

Days of the Week

Monday *måndag*
Tuesday *tisdag*
Wednesday *onsdag*
Thursday *torsdag*
Friday *fredag*
Saturday *lördag*
Sunday *sön*

Months of the Year

January *januari*
February *februari*
March *mars*
April *april*
May *maj*
June *juni*
July *juli*
August *augusti*
September *september*
October *oktober*
November *november*
December *december*
month *månad*
year *år*

Numbers

1 *en/et*
2 *två*
3 *tre*
4 *fyra*
5 *fem*
6 *sex*
7 *sju*
8 *åtta*
9 *nio*
10 *tio*
100 *hundra*
1,000 *tusen*

Ingmar Bergman's The Seventh Seal

BOOKS AND FILM

Books

The first Swedish author and playwright to receive worldwide fame was August Strindberg (1849–1912), a socio-realist writer whose work spanned over four decades and included more than 60 plays and a further 30 works of fiction and non-fiction. He has been described as 'the father of modern Swedish literature'. There is a museum (see page 40) dedicated to him at his former home at Drottninggatan 85 in the city centre.

Two Swedish writers have received the Nobel Prize for Literature, Selma Lagerlöf, the first female winner of the prize, in 1909 and Pär Lagerkvist in 1951. Lagerlöf reacted against Strindberg's realism with storytelling of legends and magic, while Lagerkvist's work reflected good and evil using characters from the Christian tradition without following the doctrines of the church.

Popular authors of more recent years are particularly found in the detective genre. It began with Maj Sjöwall and Per Wahlöö in the 1960s whose collaboration produced a series of international acclaimed detective novels. The most successful writer of this genre has been Henning Mankell who died in 2015. His books featuring protagonist Inspector Kurt Wallander were made into successful TV programmes in Sweden and the UK. Other acclaimed novelists include the late Stieg Larsson whose Millen-

nium trilogy has sold some 80 million copies worldwide and been adapted into films. In 2013 David Lagercrantz was contracted to continue the Millennium series. In the realms of spy fiction and historical novels, including the best-selling Crusade trilogy, Jan Guillou is among Sweden's most popular authors.

Two worldwide famous children's authors are Astrid Lindgren and Tove Jansson. Lindgren is best known for her *Pippi Longstocking* books and in 2013 was reportedly the third most translated children's author in the world after Hans Christian Anderson and the Brothers Grimm. Jansson, from Finland, was part of the minority Swedish-speaking population and is remembered for the much-loved *Moomin* series.

Faceless Killers by Henning Mankell. The first in the Wallander detective series by this popular author.

The Girl in the Spider's Web by David Lagercrantz. A continuation of the late Stieg Larsson's novels featuring Lisbeth Salander.

The Millenium Triology by Stieg Larsson. The man behind the tattooed misfit Lisbeth Salander and her exploits sadly died before the completion of his third novel, **The Girl Who Kicked the Hornets' Nest**.

Stockholm: A Cultural & Literary History by Tony Griffiths. An exploration of the Swedish capital old and new, revealing a city of unexpected contradictions.

Noomi Rapace and Michael Nyqvist in the original Girl With The Dragon Tattoo

Stockholm Horizons by Jeppe Wikström. This enormous, beautifully photographed volume features both the familiar and surprising aspects of Stockholm's beauty.
The Stockholm Octavo by Karen Engleman. Intriugue and political shenanigans in this novel of 18th-century Sweden.
Sweden's History in Outline by Jörgen Weibull. A detailed account, from Swedish pre-history to the age of cyberspace by way of the Vikings.
Swedish Food & Cooking by Anna Mosesson. With more than 60 delectable recipes and an overview of Swedish cuisine, this book gives a great introduction to local food.

Film

Sweden has proved the most prominent in the Scandinavian film industry and this is mainly due to the acclaimed directors Victor Sjöström and Ingmar Bergman, and more recently to Roy Andersson, Lasse Hallström (of **ABBA: The Movie** fame) and Lukas Moodysson. Sjöström was a pioneering film director, screenwriter and actor, working primarily in the silent era and moving to Hollywood in 1924, which became home to other directors, including Mauritz Stiller, and stars such as Greta Garbo. In 1957 Sjöström played the lead role in Ingmar Bergman's **Wild Strawberries**, his final performance before his death in 1960.

Ingmar Bergman is a legend in film direction, his work spanning six decades. He career started in 1941 by rewriting scripts but in the following dec-ade he wrote and directed more than a dozen films, gaining international recognition and winning numerous awards. He retired from filmmaking in 2003 at the age of 85. Although no relation, the internationally acclaimed Oscar-winning Swedish actress Ingrid Bergman did star in Bergman's **Autumn Sonata** (1978), receiving an Oscar nomination. She is however remembered more for her work with Alfred Hitchcock, working alongside Hollywood greats such as Gregory Peck and Cary Grant, and for **Casablanca** (1942) with co-star Humphrey Bogart.

Films that have been shot on location in Sweden have included two versions of Astrid Lindgren's **Pippi Longstocking** produced in 1949 and 1969. **The New Adventures of Pippi Longstocking** (1988) was, however, shot in Florida. **Mio in the Land of Faraway** (1987) based on the 1954 novel by Astrid Lindgren and starring Christopher Lee and Christian Bale was shot in English with many scenes filmed in Stockholm. The story of a boy from Stockholm who travels into a fantasy world, it was subsequently dubbed into Swedish. Other films shot in Stockholm include the Swedish versions of Stieg Larsson's trilogy (2009) and the Hollywood/Swedish version of **The Girl with Dragon Tattoo** (2011), which starred Daniel Craig.

The Swedish Film Institute was founded in 1963 to support Swedish film-making and to promote Swedish cinema internationally. It also holds the annual Guldbagge Awards.

ABOUT THIS BOOK

This *Explore Guide* has been produced by the editors of Insight Guides, whose books have set the standard for visual travel guides since 1970. With top-quality photography and authoritative recommendations, these guidebooks bring you the very best routes and itineraries in the world's most exciting destinations.

BEST ROUTES

The routes in the book provide something to suit all budgets, tastes and trip lengths. As well as covering the destination's many classic attractions, the itineraries track lesser-known sights, and there are also excursions for those who want to extend their visit outside the city. The routes embrace a range of interests, so whether you are an art fan, a gourmet, a history buff or have kids to entertain, you will find an option to suit.

We recommend reading the whole of a route before setting out. This should help you to familiarise yourself with it and enable you to plan where to stop for refreshments – options are shown in the 'Food and Drink' box at the end of each tour.

For our pick of the tours by theme, consult Recommended Routes for… (see pages 6–7).

INTRODUCTION

The routes are set in context by this introductory section, giving an overview of the destination to set the scene, plus background information on food and drink, shopping and more, while a succinct history timeline highlights the key events over the centuries.

DIRECTORY

Also supporting the routes is a Directory chapter, with a clearly organised A–Z of practical information, our pick of where to stay while you are there and select restaurant listings; these eateries complement the more low-key cafés and restaurants that feature within the routes and are intended to offer a wider choice for evening dining. Also included here are some nightlife listings, plus a handy language guide and our recommendations for books and films about the destination.

ABOUT THE AUTHORS

Jackie Staddon and Hilary Weston were delighted to be able to revisit Stockholm in preparation for this guide. They particularly enjoyed being able to walk the compact old town one day and in complete contrast take a boat to one of the islands the next. Jackie and Hilary have contributed to many other guides for Insight including *Explore Prague* and *Explore Krakow*.

CONTACT THE EDITORS

We hope you find this Explore Guide useful, interesting and a pleasure to read. If you have any questions or feedback on the text, pictures or maps, please do let us know. If you have noticed any errors or outdated facts, or have suggestions for places to include on the routes, we would be delighted to hear from you. Please drop us an email at hello@insightguides.com. Thanks!

CREDITS

Explore Stockholm
Managing Editor: Carine Tracanelli
Author: Jackie Staddon and Hilary Weston
Head of Production: Rebeka Davies
Update Production: Apa Digital
Picture Editor: Tom Smyth
Cartography: original cartography Carte

Photo credits: Photo credits: 4Corners Images 4/5T, 28/29T; Alamy 58, 70, 71, 120; Anna Gardén 59; Bengt Nyman 76/77; Berns 107; Birgersdotter 93; Björn Tesch/imagebank.sweden.se 4MC; Cecilia Larsson Lantz/Imagebank.sweden.se 41; Elias Gammelgård 106; Erik Lernestål 55, 57M; Erik Olsson 16/17, 104; Erik Wadell/Prins Eugens Waldemarsudde 52; First Hotels 90ML, 92, 100; Fredrik Nystedt/Rockfoto/imagebank.sweden.se 22/23; Getty Images 6TL, 40, 57T, 78/79, 90/91T; Helena Wahlman/imagebank. sweden.se 18; Henrik Trygg/imagebank. sweden.se 24/25, 89; Hotel Birger Jarl 90MR; Hotel Skeppsholmen 90MR; Ingalill Snitt 56; iStock 4MR, 4ML, 8MC, 14/15, 28MR, 42/43, 52/53, 54, 60/61, 62, 63L, 80T, 82B, 82T, 83L, 82/83, 85L, 116; Janus Langhorn/imagebank.sweden.se 19L; Jeanette Hägglund 56/57T; Julian Love/Apa Publications 4ML, 4MC, 4MR, 6MC, 6BC, 7M, 7MR, 8MC, 8MR, 10, 11L, 10/11, 13, 18/19, 21, 28ML, 28MC, 28MC, 30, 31L, 30/31, 32, 33M, 33T, 32/33T, 35B, 35T, 36, 37, 46, 46/47, 48, 49L, 50, 64, 65L, 64/65, 66, 72B, 74T, 76/77, 78, 79L, 80B, 81, 84, 84/85, 86, 87L, 86/87, 110, 111, 112, 113, 114, 115, 118; Karin Backlund 101; Kevin Kee Pil Cho/imagebank.sweden.se 1, 117; Lars Ekdahl/Millesgården 28ML; Leonardo 90ML, 90ML, 94, 95, 96, 97, 103; Lola Akinmade Åkerström/imagebank.sweden. se 23L; LUX Dag för Dag 90MC, 105; Martin Botvidsson/The Flyink Elk 98; Mats Bäcker 8ML, 22; Medeltidsmuseet 43M; Nobel Media AB/Alexander Mahmoud 27; Nobelmuseet 34; Ola Ericson/imagebank. sweden.se 12, 28MR, 38, 53L, 68/69, 108; Public domain 26, 44B; Pål Allan/ ABBA The Museum 7T; Sara Ingman/ imagebank.sweden.se 25L; Shutterstock 6ML, 7MR, 44/45T, 47L, 68, 72T, 73, 75; Simon Paulin/imagebank.sweden.se 39; Snap Stills/REX/Shutterstock 121; Stock Connection/REX/Shutterstock 69L; Super-Stock 8/9T, 67, 88; Susanne Walström/imagebank.sweden.se 17L; Tina Stafrén/imagebank.sweden.se 16; Tove K Breitstein/ REX/Shutterstock 74B; Tuukka Ervasti/ imagebank.sweden.se 8ML, 20, 62/63, 119; Tuukka Ervasti/imagebank.sweden. se 102, 109; vdKG Design/The Flying Elk 99; Werner Nystrand/Folio/imagebank. sweden.se 24; Åke E:son Lindman/ABBA The Museum 48/49; Åke E:son Lindman/ Prins Eugens Waldemarsudde 51

Cover credits: Shutterstock (main&bottom)

Printed by CTPS – China

DISTRIBUTION

UK, Ireland and Europe
Apa Publications (UK) Ltd
sales@insightguides.com
United States and Canada
Ingram Publisher Services
ips@ingramcontent.com
Australia and New Zealand
Woodslane; info@woodslane.com.au
Southeast Asia
Apa Publications
(Singapore) Pte
singaporeoffice@insightguides.com
Hong Kong, Taiwan and China
Apa Publications (HK) Ltd
hongkongoffice@insightguides.com

Worldwide
Apa Publications (UK) Ltd
sales@insightguides.com

SPECIAL SALES, CONTENT LICENSING AND COPUBLISHING

Insight Guides can be purchased in bulk quantities at discounted prices. We can create special editions, personalised jackets and corporate imprints tailored to your needs.
sales@insightguides.com
www.insightguides.biz

INDEX

MAP LEGEND

- ● Start of tour
- → Tour & route direction
- ❶ Recommended sight
- ❷ Recommended restaurant/café
- ★ Place of interest
- ❶ Tourist information
- ✈ Airport
- ▬ Railway
- -- Ferry route
- 🚍 Main bus station
- Ⓣ Metro station
- ✉ Main post office
- Ⅿ Museum/gallery
- ♨ Theatre
- Church
- ✡ Synagogue
- Important building
- Park
- Urban area
- Non-urban area

INSIGHT ⊙ GUIDES
OFF THE SHELF

Since 1970, INSIGHT GUIDES has provided a unique perspective on the world's best travel destinations by using specially commissioned photography and illuminating text written by local authors.

Whether you're planning a city break, a walking tour or the journey of a lifetime, our superb range of guidebooks and phrasebooks will inspire you to discover more about your chosen destination.

INSIGHT GUIDES

offer a unique combination of stunning photos, absorbing narrative and detailed maps, providing all the inspiration and information you need.

PHRASEBOOKS & DICTIONARIES

help users to feel at home, when away. Pocket-sized with a free app to download, they go where you do.

CITY GUIDES

pack hundreds of great photos into a smaller format with detailed practical information, so you can navigate the world's top cities with confidence.

EXPLORE GUIDES

feature easy-to-follow walks and itineraries in the world's most exciting destinations, with our choice of the best places to eat and drink along the way.

POCKET GUIDES

combine concise information on where to go and what to do in a handy compact format, ideal on the ground. Includes a full-colour, fold-out map.

EXPERIENCE GUIDES

feature offbeat perspectives and secret gems for experienced travellers, with a collection of over 100 ideas for a memorable stay in a city.

www.insightguides.com